SCRUM For The Rest Of Us!
A Braintrust Field Guide

BY BRIAN M. RABON, CST, PMP

Design by The Modern Brand Company, agency of record for The Braintrust Consulting Group since 2008. themodernbrand.com

First published by Dog Ear Publishing
4010 W. 86th Street, Ste H
Indianapolis, IN 46268
www.dogearpublishing.net

ISBN: 978-1-4575-2580-3

Printed in the United States of America

CONTENTS

DEDICATION

There is a saying "it takes a village to raise a child"; that is particularly true for the development of our company, Braintrust, and this book. You wouldn't be reading this book today if it wasn't for the efforts (more like blood, sweat, and tears) of many wonderful individuals. I dedicate this book to the entire Braintrust Team and to our supporters:

Kate and Dan, my business partners. Thank you for being there for me every day. Even when times get tough, I always know you have my back.

John, Lonnie, and Erick for helping delight our clients and transform so many organizations

Kristyn and Scott for helping us define our sales voice and providing such great service to our customers

Kim and Tess for supporting all of us while in the field

My Agile/Scrum mentors—Dave, Jimmy, Lyssa, Michele, and Tom— thank you so very much for helping me when I needed it most

Paul McGuire for helping me get this book started

My business mentor, Dale—if it wasn't for you pushing me out of the nest, I wouldn't have founded Braintrust

My family—Mom (Judy), Dad (Charles), Jonathan, Megan, and Adam

My wife, Elizabeth, my greatest supporter and lifelong friend and confidant (I LOVE YOU "E"!)

DEDICATION

Before this group of talented individuals got hold of my manuscript, it was full of typos, bad grammar, and lots of hard to read sentences. A special thank you to the following people who gave their time to make this a better book: Darlena Battle, Sarenna "Cocoa B" Benjamin, Jeffrey "Jeff" Van Brunt, Balagee Govindan, Mark Kilby, Paxton Lamons, Stephen Maldony, Fred Mastropasqua, Lynn Mettler, John Miller, Jill Moller, John Pruitt, Jerry Rajamoney, Marat Rikelman, Thomas Soltau, John Stenbeck, Ken Sawyer, and Andrew Webster. You guys rock. Thank you so very much!

A special thanks to my professional editor, Lauren Mix, for putting the final polish on this book.

Last, but not least, I dedicate this book to all of you who are in the trenches every day struggling to make things better at your organization. Please never give up or stop fighting the good fight. You can do it!

PREFACE

As this is a book on Scrum, an Agile method, I thought it appropriate to start off with a User Story...

> *"As an individual interested in Scrum,*
> *I want practical, real-world advice on Scrum,*
> *so that I can be successful at understanding and practicing Scrum."*

Now, let's deconstruct this User Story...

"As A..."—Who Is This Book For

The "As a" line of a User Story speaks of who the feature is for. I asked my Team of reviewers to share who they thought would benefit from reading this book. They came up with the following groups of individuals:

> *"I feel that anyone with an interest in Scrum, particularly at the beginning or intermediate level, would benefit from reading the book."*
> *—Ken Sawyer*

> *"Any member of any product development Team, specifically organizations interested in adapting a new methodology to serve customers better and faster."—Marat Rikelman*

> *"I see 2 audiences: Beginners needing a quick overview of Scrum and seasoned professionals needing a quick reference, especially when meeting with Stakeholders so they can give real-life, easy to understand definitions."—Stephen Maldony*

If you are new to Scrum and want to learn it quickly or are a veteran who occasionally needs a quick reference, this book is for you.

"I Want..."—What Are You Looking For?

While it can be arrogant to make assumptions about why people would want to read a book, it must be written with a particular target audience in mind. Here is what I was thinking about when I set out to write this book.

Since founding Braintrust years ago, I have been working with thousands of individuals at hundreds of organizations to successfully implement Agile/Scrum. I have had the privilege of seeing Scrum done really well, but have also had the misfortune of seeing it done poorly too many times.

Often, people come to me with an incorrect or biased view of Scrum. Perhaps they were never formally trained, or were trained by a biased, internally developed class. These individuals are always shocked to learn what Scrum is and I love seeing the light bulb come on for them. Sometimes just knowing what Scrum actually is can be enough to help someone succeed.

During every class or coaching engagement I come across deep questions and people who have complex issues needing resolution. I have captured some of these questions and provided solid guidance from actual client solutions in the Questions and Answers and Smells sections.

Rather than devoting your life to teaching/coaching Scrum, like I have for the past years, learn from my experiences with countless clients and their solutions.

Ever wonder why someone would take the time to author a book? Especially a book on a well-known subject, such as Scrum? After having read the majority of the Scrum books on the market today, I have come to the conclusion that many of them focus on software development. My vision for writing this book is to author a text applicable to any field. Whether you are applying Scrum for hardware development, running your non-profit, teaching school, or tackling a home improvement effort, the knowledge in this book still applies.

So what makes this book non-software development specific?

> No **Technobabble.** It is written in plain English, with the simplest explanations possible.
>
> After having trained and coached thousands of people at hundreds of organizations, I have seen what works across many different fields and am presenting those findings to you.
>
> Regardless of what field you are in, this book specifically points out areas that may challenge you and your organization with adopting Scrum.
>
> Other books point out challenges with implementing Scrum, but they stop there. This book goes one step further and gives practical solutions to your most challenging issues.

If you find that this User Story...

> *"As an individual interested in Scrum,*
> *I want practical real-world advice on Scrum,*
> *so that I can be successful at understanding and practicing Scrum."*

...fits your situation, then it is my hope this book will help you to be more successful with applying Scrum. Only one person can be the judge of whether or not I have accomplished my goal and that would be you.

Please contact me at brian.rabon@braintrustgroup.com or 205.329.3974 and let me know if this book works for you.

Sincerely,

Brian Rabon

Brian M. Rabon, CST, PMP

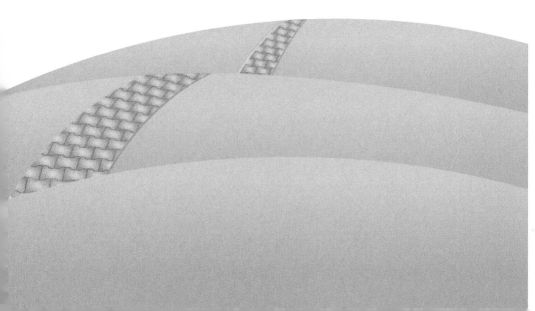

HOW TO USE THIS BOOK

If you have picked up this book, you obviously have more than a passing interest in Agile/Scrum. Perhaps you are new to Agile/Scrum, have heard a few buzzwords, but the core concepts are not familiar yet. Perhaps you are an Agile/Scrum veteran who wants to brush up on their knowledge. Regardless of where you are on your path to mastery, this guide will help you to gain more understanding and knowledge.

This guide is broken up into several sections:

Introduction—An explanation of what Agile is and how is it different from Scrum, the features and benefits of Scrum, and thoughts behind how this "way to get work done" works

Roles In Scrum—Who the key players are in Scrum and what they are responsible for

Meetings (Ceremonies) In Scrum—The Sprint and all the core meetings that make it up

Artifacts In Scrum—What is left behind, in terms of documentation, after a Sprint is complete

Conclusion—My parting thoughts and a glossary chock-full of terms to help you understand Scrum better

Throughout the guide you will notice a lot of **bold, *italicized*** words. Whenever you see one of these, check the glossary at the back of the book to find an in-depth definition.

You can read this book cover-to-cover or simply jump to the section you need help with most. Remember to keep this guide close-at-hand and you will always be in-the-know.

WHAT'S MISSING FROM THIS BOOK?

The following topics can be very important to making Scrum work properly, but have been left out of this guide on purpose. It was my intention to make this guide succinct enough to read in one trans-continental flight. Also, I wanted to focus on topics core to Scrum and so there are certain Generally Accepted Scrum Practices (GASPs) that won't be included. Here is the list...

User Stories

    Acceptance Criteria

    Epics

    Sizing (Relative Estimation)

Scaling Scrum

The Work Of The Product Owner

    Prioritizing

    Strategic Planning in Scrum

        Visioning

        Road-Mapping

        Release Planning

Now, if you can't wait for my next book to come out on these GASPs, then perhaps you can find some answers in the following resources:

Agile Atlas—http://www.agileatlas.org

Agile Product Management With Scrum—Roman Pichler, 978-0321605788

User Stories Applied—Mike Cohn, 978-0321205681

You can always checkout our company Blog—http://www.braintrustgroup.com/blog as well!

INTRODUCTION

WHAT'S AHEAD IN THIS SECTION

What is Agile

Agile outside of software development

An overview of Scrum

What makes Agile tick and how it differs from traditional methods

The features and benefits of Scrum

When to apply Scrum

Agile, An Overview

Many of you will already be familiar with a plan-driven method of getting work done, such as **Waterfall**. You may be less familiar with an iterative-incremental development method like Scrum, which is considered to be Agile. If you already familiar with why Scrum is considered an Agile method, feel free to skip this section, if not, read on for a brief history lesson.

The term **Agile,** as applied to an alternative way of developing software, was coined in February of 2001. Frustrated with the prevailing software development paradigms, a group of 17 met and hashed out a powerful statement of why they felt there needed to be change in a document called **The Agile Manifesto.** The Agile Manifesto can be found at http://www.agilemanifesto.org, and an in-depth look at the Manifesto can be found in our article on the *Core Values of Agile* (http://www.braintrustgroup.com/2012/the-agile-manifesto-reviewing-agiles-core-values).

The Manifesto has become a statement of values and principles about what Agile development should look like. Collaboration, accepting change, interacting face-to-face, and a functional product are valued over pre-defined plans, documentation, and rigid processes. Agile is sometimes referred to as a lightweight process because of the lack of formal steps and planning documentation. Just because these components are not overly emphasized does not mean they are absent. Instead, they're tailored to meet the needs of the effort without compromising Agile's core values.

The primary features of Agile support continuous improvement and innovation of the **Product**. Instead of clearly defining every detail of the Product prior to starting work, Agile focuses on setting a **Vision** and outlining details with incremental development of small pieces of functionality. Thus, a **Stakeholder** can suggest new ideas along the way, with minimal disruption to work already performed on the Product.

Agile is a philosophy or mindset for iterative and incremental Product development, based upon a shared set of values and principles. The implementations of Agile promote Teamwork, collaboration, and adaptability throughout the lifecycle of Product development. There are approximately forty methods considered Agile for developing Products. Some examples include: Scrum, Extreme Programming (XP), Kanban/Lean, Crystal, Feature Driven Development (FDD).

So, what is the connection between Agile and Scrum again? I like to think of Agile as the generic (think tissues) and Scrum as the brand name (think Kleenex). Put another way, Scrum has a specific way of implementing generic Agile concepts. For example, Agile calls for work to be completed in short periods of time called **Iterations**, while Scrum implements Iterations with the concept of **Sprints**. It also shares the same values and principles as all Agile methods.

Thinking Bigger (Agile Outside of Software Development)

When the founding fathers of Agile wrote The Agile Manifesto, they originally wanted to find a way to improve their software development. The question today is, "Were the founding fathers of Agile thinking big enough?" With time, Agile has evolved beyond software development and is now used to manage work in all sorts of industries. Here are just a few examples:

Eric Reis with his book "The Lean Entrepreneur" has revolutionized the way startups and venture capitalists work today

Joe Justice is taking on the "Big-Three" automakers with his car company Wikispeed (http://wikispeed.com)

James Denning with his book "The Leader's Guide to Radical Management" is transforming business management as we know it

Braintrust's very own John Miller is adapting Scrum for use in K-12 education (http://theagileschool.blogspot.com)

This book has intentionally been written to leave out references to software development. While still relevant to software development, this guide will just as easily help you plan your next marketing campaign, your next vacation, or even help you get your chores done in your household.

SCRUM, AN OVERVIEW

Fundamentally, Scrum is a "way to get work done". It is based on the concept of "KISS" (Keep It Simple, Stupid.) by only specifying a few concepts and letting you and your organization fill in the gaps. Scrum is considered an Agile method because the values and principles of the Agile Manifesto can be found throughout. Scrum is also based on its own set of values: commitment, focus, openness, respect, and courage. According to a VersionOne survey (1), Scrum is the most popular of the Agile Methods. The following paragraphs will give a brief overview of Scrum, which will then be detailed over the next several chapters.

In Scrum, there are 3 primary roles: the **Team**, a group of individuals who get the work done, the **Product Owner**, who represents the Stakeholders' desires to the Team, and the **ScrumMaster**, who focuses on helping the Team maximize their productivity through constant improvement. Everyone else is considered a Stakeholder and their input is valued and needed throughout the process.

Everyone's ideas for the Product go into what we call the **Product Backlog**. You can think of the Product Backlog as an iceberg, a dynamic entity. New ideas are constantly coming in and old ideas are falling off the bottom, melting away. The Product Owner maintains the Product Backlog; taking in new ideas, refining existing ideas, and always keeping it in priority order, based on everyone's feedbac'

The Stakeholders want to get the Product built and we accomplish this through executing one or more Sprints. A **Sprint** is a period of time (typically 2 to 4 weeks) at the end of which we expect to have a **Potentially Shippable Product Increment** (a functional piece of the Product).

The Sprint starts with a **Sprint Planning** meeting revolving around 2 primary conversations. The first conversation is the Product Owner presenting the highest **Priority** Product Backlog Items to the Team and the Team deciding which ones they are comfortable getting **Done**. The second part of the conversation involves the Team getting technical and figuring out the Tasks necessary to get the agreed upon Product **Backlog Items** complete. Once the goal and the scope of the Sprint is set, the Team is ready to start building.

The heartbeat of each Sprint is the **Daily Scrum** meeting. This meeting is an opportunity for the Team to come together briefly to discuss their progress, ask for help, and synchronize their efforts. We may also incorporate other tools during the Sprint, in order to promote **transparency**, like **Burn-Down Charts** and **Scrum Boards** (discussed in greater detail later in this text).

At the end of the Sprint, it's time to **Inspect** and **Adapt** in order to improve. First, we Inspect and Adapt the Product in a meeting called the **Sprint Review**. This is an opportunity to invite the Stakeholders in, give them a demo, and seek their feedback. The feedback from this meeting becomes new Product Backlog Items put into the Product Backlog for future consideration.

After the Sprint Review meeting, we thank the Stakeholders for attending and the Scrum Team (Team, Product Owner, and ScrumMaster) meets in order to Inspect and Adapt the process in a Sprint Retrospective (retro). During the retro, the Scrum Team reflects on how they worked together, focusing on what worked well and what needs to change to improve the Team. At the conclusion of the retro, the Scrum Team leaves the room with specific, actionable next steps that, when implemented in the next iteration, will improve their performance as a Team.

The output of every Sprint is a Potentially Shippable Product Increment, another brick in the proverbial wall. The decision of whether to give this functionality to the Stakeholders then becomes a business decision made by the Product Owner.

Sprints continue, one after the other, until the Product Owner calls the development effort Done. This can happen when a targeted date has been reached, the budget has been depleted, or enough **Business Value** has been delivered to meet the needs of the Stakeholders.

Got it? Not quite? That's ok; we will spend the remainder of this book getting into detail about the intricacies of the Scrum Process.

(1) Version One "The State of Agile Development" 7th Annual Survey: 2013

HOW IS SCRUM DIFFERENT?

Many of us are used to working in a more traditional, plan-driven environment. When we develop a new Product, we first meet with our Stakeholders and gather requirements. We then review those requirements and decide which ones to build, or baseline our scope. Next, we meet with our Team to plan the development effort. Once everyone agrees to the plan, we start executing the plan and monitoring and controlling the progress along the way. In the end, we deliver the finished product to the Stakeholder to their delight and all live happily ever after, right?

Unfortunately our Product development efforts rarely, if ever, go this smoothly. It seems that our Stakeholders don't really know what they want or change their minds halfway through. When this happens, it interrupts the Team's flow and we have to re-plan. Or perhaps the Team encounters a technical difficulty while building some feature and they get behind schedule. I am sure that we have all had some type of Product development failure in the past and the reasons are too numerous to name here.

What makes Scrum different from the traditional plan-driven approach? Think of a Scrum Team as a bunch of researchers following the scientific method; they develop a hypothesis, design experiments to test the hypothesis, execute the tests then evaluate the results of their experiment with the Stakeholders. If the Stakeholders are happy with the Teams' progress, they keep going. If they didn't get what they want, they make a new hypothesis and run another experiment in a future iteration. It's trial and error at its finest, in a controlled and structured way.

Scrum focuses on planning on a micro-scale, only detailing the piece of the product about to be implemented. We build a little bit at a time, constantly seeking Stakeholder feedback. These practices eliminate most of the risk with developing a new Product and since the new functionality is ready at regular intervals, we are able to deliver value back to the Stakeholders more frequently.

Because of the incremental iterative nature, we consider Scrum to be an Empirical development method. Whereas the traditional, plan-driven approach, is considered defined. In order for an Empirical method, such as Scrum, to be successful, we need to consider three things:

> **Transparency**—make it visible, we can't evaluate what we cannot see

> **Inspection**—take time out, frequently, to see how things are going

> **Adaptation**—when things get off course, make changes to bring them back

Now that you know the essence of what makes Scrum tick; don your lab coat, grab your Team, and go build something truly innovative for your Stakeholders. Remember to keep things visible and be sure to inspect and adapt your Product and your process frequently.

Next, we will look at the features and benefits of Scrum. Why would I include these sections? Many of my clients are faced with introducing Scrum into their working environments. They are often challenged with getting buy-in and educating everyone on the value of the approach, yet many of them are not trained salespeople. Here is your one minute sales lesson for the day; we buy benefits, but it's the features that typically sell a product. Knowing the features and benefits of Scrum can help you form more compelling arguments for why it should be implemented within your environment. Sales lesson over, read on for the features and benefits!

FEATURES OF SCRUM

Why Scrum is so popular? Below are the features of Scrum that have made it the most popular Agile method for developing Products. Understanding the features can help you decide if Scrum is right for your organization.

Features of Scrum From The Client Perspective

Too many Product development efforts get caught up in the overhead of administration, delays in shipping due to poorly-written requirements, and subpar Products meeting only minimal requirements (if that), disappointing Stakeholders. Below are the features of Scrum that will help you create "wow" moments for your clients. Remember, ultimately, Product Delivery is about satisfying the Stakeholders.

Delight your Stakeholders by building exactly what they want, even if those wants change throughout the process.

Quickly deliver the most important features first, thus supporting your Stakeholders by delivering value in short cycles.

Adapt to meet the current business need by prioritizing Tasks.

Embrace change in order to better meet true business needs.

Features of Scrum From The Organization Perspective

Satisfied Stakeholders, who demand your products, are the lifeblood of your business. A repeatable process that delivers products meeting this demand is like having a goose that lays golden eggs. In this sense, the features of Scrum below will benefit your organization.

Builds continuous innovation

Creates order out of chaos

Has a positive impact on the culture of the organization; as Scrum spreads, other areas of your business may choose to adopt the values and principles of Agile as well.

Features of Scrum From The Management Perspective

According to Scrum founding father Mike Cohn, the purpose of management in Scrum is to define containers, differences, and exchanges. Creating this type of environment fosters self-organization and self-management, freeing leaders up from having to be so tactically focused to being more strategic.

Subtle control of the work shift from management to the Team; the Team is now responsible for continually producing small parts of a larger working Product

A better Team understanding of how much work they can do in a given timeframe

An environment where the Team can find ways to solve their own issues and problems

Features of Scrum From The Product Perspective

In the Agile framework, Products move along the development pipeline faster. The unique nature of the Sprint in Scrum's framework ensures that a version of the Product is always ready to ship. Scrum's other features as referenced to the Product prove that:

Due to collaboration, your Product gets better over time.

Due to the real-time Inspect-and-Adapt loop, the Team is able to deliver exactly what is needed.

The Product becomes more valuable because it does exactly what the Stakeholders want it to do.

Scrum provides early feedback on your Product.

Scrum supports predictability of your development process.

Because the Team delivers a Potentially Shippable Product Increment every Sprint, there is always a shippable Product. In the worst case, we revert only a single Sprint's worth of development if a Sprint is a failure.

Features of Scrum From The Team Perspective

With all of the self-managing aspects of Scrum, your Team will discover newfound autonomy in the execution of their development. The features of Scrum your Team will find appealing are:

It is more fun to be on a Scrum Team

Increased ownership of the work they have done

Collaboration with Team Members to learn other areas of working the Product

BENEFITS OF SCRUM

There is a subtle but tangible difference between features and benefits. Basically, a Stakeholder uses features, but buys the benefits. The same is true for adopting a project management process. Before you decide to overhaul your project management office and implement something like Scrum, you need to know how your organization will benefit. This section looks to identify those benefits of Scrum that have made it the most popular Agile method for developing Products.

Benefits of Scrum From The Client Perspective

Though a Stakeholder really doesn't care about the project management process the Team uses, they do realize some benefits from it. Scrum provides a definite set of benefits over the traditional methods and over other Agile methodologies. For the client, the benefits of Scrum are:

Scrum puts the control of the **Value Stream** (the value-added steps of the development process) back in the hands of the business.

Scrum allows clients to easily change **Priorities** and needs.

At regular intervals, the client is able to inspect the work that is done and decide whether they like it or even if they want to keep investing in the Product development effort. This practice limits the client exposure therefore decreasing the risk of the precious capital investment.

Benefits of Scrum From The Organization Perspective

As an organization, it is a big decision to adopt a new process like Agile. It is often a culture change so it's important to see tangible benefits quickly. This is where Scrum shines. With a predictable, repeatable release schedule and Self-Managing Teams, the organization realizes the following benefits:

Scrum keeps an organization honest and helps them meet their commitments.

Scrum promotes transparency; you no longer need to hide the truth, you can be open and honest with everyone.

Decision making is shifted to the lowest level (line employees), the best people who are able to understand all of the facts.

Benefits of Scrum From The Management Perspective

Management, the decision-makers within the organization, will enjoy some benefit as well. The predictable development process provides them with such benefits as:

Better workforce management

Enhanced Stakeholder relationships

Visibility into the entirety of the project management process

Motivated and inspired Team members

Benefits of Scrum From The Product Perspective

The lifecycle of the product will be improved by the Scrum process, which leads to the following Product-related benefits:

Improved credibility with your Stakeholders due to a higher quality Product

More predictable release cycles with built-in testing processes, leading to better Product stability

Using the Sprint Review naturally leads to a Product that the client wants and is excited about

Benefits of Scrum From The Team Perspective

In the end, the Team will enjoy benefits of Scrum that reinforce their best work. Autonomy, self-direction, immediate feedback, and true collaboration lead to such benefits for the Team such as:

Increased satisfaction with work

True potential of the Team unlocked

A safe working environment where people can thrive

A learned, sustainable pace supporting a high level of productivity over the long-haul

WHEN TO USE SCRUM

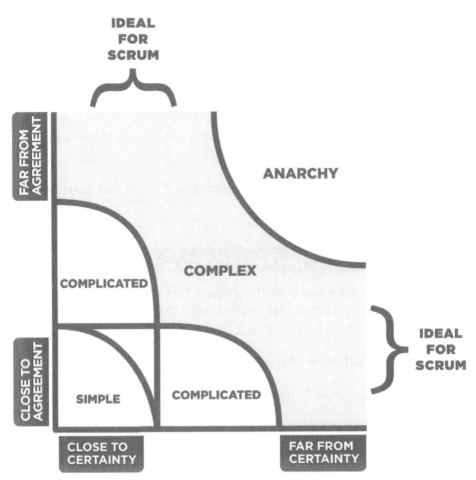

I am a pragmatist; I don't believe that there is a one-size-fits-all solution to developing Products. Scrum is a great way to get work done, but it may not be appropriate for all situations. So when should you apply Scrum and when should you use an alternate method? There are several factors to consider:

Where are you in the ideation of your Product?

Still in R&D—too early for Scrum

Know what you want, but missing the details—ideal for Scrum

Known quantity, time to mass produce—too late for Scrum

How well known are the requirements of your Stakeholders?

> No clue, they can't agree—too early for Scrum

> There is some disagreement, but they have some common needs—ideal for Scrum

> They are airtight, everyone agreed to them up-front—not ideal for Scrum

Does the Team know how to solve the problem?

> They are completely lost, seems like you just asked them to put a man on Mars—not ideal for Scrum

> They have some reasonable ideas and experience with the solutions—ideal for Scrum

> They already have it sorted and are well versed in the solution—not ideal for Scrum

Scrum is best applied when we haven't fully developed the Product yet, requirements are still not clear, and the solution hasn't been completely hashed out. You can apply Scrum in these other areas, but expect to modify Scrum to make it fit your situation.

INTRODUCTION SUMMARY—WHERE WE HAVE BEEN

> We looked at Agile and how it relates to Scrum

> We saw how Agile is being applied outside of Software Development

> We took a brief tour of Scrum and why it works

> We learned the key features and benefits of Scrum to help us sell it within our organization

> Finally, we saw when to apply Scrum to be most successful

ROLES IN SCRUM

WHAT'S AHEAD IN THIS SECTION?

Team Members

Product Owner

ScrumMaster

Servant Leadership

Stakeholders

Pigs and chickens, oh my!

Team Member

Team Member is one of the 3 roles on a Scrum Team. You can think of the **Team**

Member as someone who does the work of developing the Product. A Team is ideally comprised of 5 to 9 members (7 +/- 2). The three primary characteristics of the Team are that they are **Cross-Functional**—diverse skill sets on the Team, **Self-Organizing**—everyone decides what type of work they would like to do, and **Self-Managing**—they decide their own tasks and the order in which to accomplish them.

For broader definition of these terms check the glossary in the back of the book.

Traits of An Effective Team Member

"T-Shaped" person; someone who has deep knowledge in one or two areas, but is also skilled across multiple domains (a Specializing Generalist)

Craftsperson who is a career professional and takes pride in doing quality work

Team player who enjoys the camaraderie of working with others on challenging problems

An open individual who is willing to share the honest truth (the good, bad, and the ugly) of how they are doing at all times

Someone who isn't afraid to ask for help when they need it

Key Attitude

"I do my work and I do it well, but my race isn't won until all my fellow Team Members cross the finish line with me. We win as a Team. I check my title (as well as my ego) at the door; I am willing to do whatever it takes to help the Team succeed, even if that means working outside of my area of expertise or comfort zone."—Team Member

How The Team Members Participate In The Sprint

Team Members are involved in every step of the Sprint. During the 1st half of Sprint Planning (the "What" conversation), Team Members work with the Product Owner to select Product Backlog Items from the overall Product Backlog. They select an appropriate amount of work by comparing their historical **Velocity** with the number of **Story Points** previously assigned to each Product Backlog Item. Then, during the 2nd half of Sprint Planning (the "How" conversation), the Team Members create **Tasks** (the Sprint Backlog) from the Product Backlog Items chosen in the "What" meeting. The Tasks are all the steps necessary to take a Product Backlog Item from concept to reality (**Production Ready**), typically estimated in **Ideal Hours**.

After the Team completes the Sprint Planning Meeting, they enter the heart of the Sprint, where they largely become Self-Organizing and Self-Managing. This means they conduct the Daily Scrum meetings with minimal assistance from the Product Owner or ScrumMaster, except, as needed, to clarify requirements and when to call a Backlog Item Done. As Team Members complete Tasks from the Sprint Backlog, they update the Burn-Down Chart and move tasks along the Scrum Board, if used.

At the conclusion of the Sprint's **Timebox**, the Team Members accompany the Product Owner and ScrumMaster to the Sprint Review meeting. Here, the Team Members demonstrate the new Product Increment for the Stakeholders and provide input and feedback to help make the Product better. Finally, the Team Members conduct a Sprint Retrospective meeting where they Inspect their process and Adapt it for improved performance during the next Sprint.

Team Q & A

Q: Where does the Team come from?
A: Management typically selects the Team.

Q: What happens when the Team grows to more than 9 members?
A: Communication paths on a Team increase via a formula $n(n-1)/2$ (36 communications paths on a Team of 9), when you add more than 9 people you begin to push the envelope of effective and efficient intra-Team communication. It is likely time to split the Team. Note that splitting the Team now requires you to scale Scrum. Scaling Scrum has its own set of challenges, which are a bit outside th scope of this book.

Smells (Problems For the Team)

Smell: Not having a truly Cross-Functional Team. For instance, quality assurance/control still resides in a separate group/silo, slowing down development and effecting Sprint completion time.

Solution: In order to be as efficient as possible, a Team needs everyone necessary to accomplish the work on the Team itself. That also means that Team members should be encouraged to wear multiple hats and help out in areas where there are bottlenecks (E.g. A developer should be willing to put on their testing hat towards the end of the Sprint).

Smell: Team Members are required to work on multiple Scrum Teams and are complaining about attending too many meetings and never getting any work done.

Solution: It is hard to be Agile when trying to balance too many separate plates at a time. Create dedicated Teams with full-time Team Members.

Smell: There are too many "Type-A" personalities on the Team. They are constantly fighting to get their way. The Team is constantly feeling the pains of interpersonal conflict.

Solution: Create awareness for the "Type-A" personalities of what they are doing and the impact it is having on the Team. This is best done in private. Let them know that Scrum is a Team sport and that they need to be willing to be a Team player.

Smell: A Team Member is not carrying their weight because they either refuse to work outside their skill set or are always picking the "easy" tasks. The rest of the Team notices this and is getting frustrated with the individual. The Team has given up trying to get the Team Member to change and is ready to ask the individual to leave the Team.

Solution: The ScrumMaster, in a one-on-one setting, should perform a root cause analysis (we like the five "Why's" Technique - keeping asking "Why" five times in a row, thinking like a two year old), to see why the Team Member is not contributing. They may need additional training or a formal reprimand from human resources depending on the circumstance.

Product Owner

The Product Owner is one of the three roles on a Scrum Team. Most notably the Product Owner serves as the liaison between the Team and the Stakeholders. To the Team, the Product Owner is the voice of the Stakeholders, representing their needs, wants, and desires for the Product.

The Product Owner has strategic oversight of the Product from the organization's perspective and owns the **Return On Investment (ROI)** for the Product. They are involved in Product planning through **Visioning, Road-Mapping**, and **Release Planning**. In general, the Product Owner works with Stakeholders and project sponsors to perform strategic planning.

The Product Owner is also responsible for the Product Backlog. They own it, maintain it, and Prioritize it (Note: Some say that the Product Backlog is **Ordered**, not Prioritized). They always assure that the needs of the Stakeholders are being best presented to the Team for implementation within the Sprints.

Traits of An Effective Product Owner

Loves to communicate, communicate, communicate

Able to see the big picture

Adept and nimble at navigating the political waters

Holds admiration and respect from the key Stakeholders (Don't worry this takes time to develop)

Has a passion for the Product and markets and sells it to everyone

Willing to make decisions at the last responsible moment

Likes to spend time with the Team and answer their questions

Not afraid to get into the weeds from time-to-time

Key Attitude

"I own this Product and I want to see it succeed. I will only ask the Team to build what has Business Value and an ROI for my organization. I am a consensus builder and I love marketing and selling the value of what the Team has accomplished."—Product Owner

How The Product Owner Participates In The Sprint

At the tactical level, the Product Owner is involved in all phases of the Sprint. During the first half of Sprint Planning (the "What" conversation), the Product Owner presents the highest priority Product Backlog Items to the Team. As owner of the Product Backlog, the Product Owner has set the priorities of the Product Backlog to match the needs of the business prior to this meeting. This allows the Team Members to effectively choose the right items from the Product Backlog to create the Sprint Backlog and accomplish the highest and best value for the Stakeholders.

The Product Owner participates in the Daily Scrum meetings to help clarify requirements and answer other questions as needed. As Team Members complete items from the Sprint Backlog, the Product Owner reviews them to provide real-time feedback and assess Doneness.

At the conclusion of the Sprint, the Product Owner accompanies the Team Members and ScrumMaster to the Sprint Review meeting. During the Sprint Review, the Product Owner reiterates the Product Vision and Roadmap. The Product Owner also continues to refine the Product backlog so it accurately reflects the feedback and ideas revealed during the review. After the Sprint Review, the Product Owner joins the rest of the Scrum Team for the Sprint Retrospective, where they share their ideas about how the entire Team can work more effectively and efficiently.

In summary, the Product Owner is the strategic interface between the Scrum Team and the Stakeholders. They own the business relationships, determine Product direction, and have responsibility for the ROI of the Product.

Product Owner Q & A

Q: Where does the Product Owner come from?
A: The best Product Owners come from the Business side of the house and are authorized by management to make decisions on their behalf.

Q: Our Product Owner is our Business Analyst, is that ok?
A: Having a Business Analyst as a Product Owner is better than not having a Product owner at all, but it is not ideal. Business Analysts may lack the big picture and spend too much time in the details to be as effective as a true business Product Owner.

Q: What happens when we don't have the support of the business and they won't give us a Product Owner?
A: Run away? Seriously, it can take time to win the support of the business. The ScrumMaster should spend time educating management on the need for the business to provide a dedicated Product Owner and explain the benefits they will receive for their investment.

Smells (Problems for the Product Owner Role)

Smell: The Product Owner is being asked to play a dual role. They have their regular, full-time functional role as well as the duties of being a Product Owner. This causes the Product Owner to be absent and unavailable a lot of the time.

Solution: Make a case for why the Product Owner is a full-time role within the organization. Once the Product Owner is freed up from their functional duties, they can then focus on working with the Team more frequently.

Smell: The Product Owner is surprised by what the Team has developed in the Sprint Review meeting. Because of this, they rarely sign-off on the Sprint Backlog Items until the subsequent Sprint. (A symptom of this happening is overly aggressive Acceptance Criteria.)

Solution: Coach the Product Owner to be more engaged during the development process itself. They should be involved throughout development, especially during the Sprint, and should feel free to give their input along the way.

Smell: The Product Owner is playing their role well, but their decisions are constantly being over-ruled by the Stakeholders. The Team is getting frustrated and they are calling the Product Owner a "lame duck".

Solution: Meet with the Stakeholders to determine why they feel the need to overrule the Product Owner. Is it because the Product Owner isn't involving them in the process? Is it that the Product Owner has lost respect from the Stakeholders? Is it that the Stakeholders are just jerks? Once the root cause has been established, take the appropriate actions necessary to improve the situation. Again, the Product Owner should be the liaison between the Stakeholders and the Team.

ScrumMaster

The ScrumMaster is the final of the 3 roles on a Scrum Team. If one sentence were used to sum up the duties of the ScrumMaster, it is that they facilitate the Scrum process as a **_Servant Leader_** (someone who leads by first taking care of other's needs). A ScrumMaster works hand-in-hand with the Product Owner to act as an Information Radiator to the Stakeholders and clears Roadblocks out of the Team's way.

The ScrumMaster serves to help the Team Members effectively engage the Sprint and the entire Scrum process. While the ScrumMaster is not the manager of the Team Members, they do serve to guide the Team in their execution of the Scrum process.

Traits of An Effective ScrumMaster

Humble, with no need to take credit for the Team's work. They get all their satisfaction from seeing them succeed.

Servant Leader who puts the needs of the Team ahead of theirs and is willing to do what it takes to help them succeed.

Diligently pursues any obstacle blocking the Team's progress and will not stop until the obstacle is removed.

Advocates for the Team, Product Owner, and the Scrum process throughout the organization.

Loyal to the Team, the Product, and the Organization.

Key Attitude

"I don't succeed unless the Team succeeds. My mission in life is to grease the wheels and ensure that everyone is playing nice and that the process is running smoothly."—ScrumMaster

How The ScrumMaster Participates In The Sprint

During the first half of Sprint Planning (The "What" conversation), the ScrumMaster works with the Product Owner and Team Members to facilitate the selection of an appropriate amount of Product Backlog Items (based on the Teams historical Velocity) from the Product Backlog that will be included in the Sprint. Then, during the second half of Sprint Planning (The "How" conversation), the ScrumMaster serves as advisor and coach to assist the Team Members with decomposing the Sprint Backlog Items into Tasks and Estimating the effort required for those Tasks. At this time, the ScrumMaster looks at Team capacity to make sure that they aren't over-committing.

The ScrumMaster participates in the Daily Scrum meetings only to the extent that the Team Members need. The primary added value for the ScrumMaster during the Daily Scrum meetings is to clear any roadblocks or obstacles that are impeding the Team's progress. As Team Members complete Product Backlog Items from the Sprint Backlog, they update the **Burn-Down Chart** and move Tasks along the Scrum Board, if used. The ScrumMaster may also facilitate this process if needed to assist the Team Members.

Once all of the Sprint Backlog Items have been completed, the ScrumMaster accompanies the Product Owner and Team Members to the Sprint Review meeting. The ScrumMaster takes a backseat to the Team and the Product Owner during the Sprint Review, helping out when needed. After the Sprint Review, the ScrumMaster facilitates the **Sprint Retrospective**, where they help the Team focus in on what is needed to improve their performance for the next Sprint.

So, while it may appear that the ScrumMaster has no real power or authority, their role is no less important to the success of the Team. Clearing Roadblocks along the way can save a typical Scrum Team many hours per Sprint. The guide and facilitator roles played by the ScrumMaster ensure that the Team runs as smoothly as possible.

ScrumMaster Q & A

Q: The ScrumMaster should be the Project Manager or Team Lead right?
A: While many ScrumMasters come from roles like Project Manager or Team Lead, they don't have to. The best candidate for ScrumMaster is someone who qualified to fulfill the position and is motivated to help the Team succeed.

Q: Can the ScrumMaster serve multiple Teams at one time?
A: Can you brush your teeth, fix your hair, and drive to work at the same time? The more Teams that one ScrumMaster serves, the less effective they will be in their role. The one caveat to this is mature Teams. Once a Team is firing on all cylinders, they may not need as much time and attention from their ScrumMaster. In this case, the ScrumMaster can look for another Team to help or may turn their focus to coaching others in their organization. Here is a table from one of my reviewers, Mark Kilby, that might help you decide what to do:

Scenario	What The ScrumMaster Should Do
If the Team or the ScrumMaster is new	ScrumMaster should focus on their one and only Team
The Team is stabilizing (Holding a steady Velocity and able to make occasional improvements on their own)	ScrumMaster could start a new Team
The Team is mature (They can run their own Sprint Retrospectives and only need occasional help from the ScrumMaster on tough problems)	ScrumMaster could start a new Team
The ScrumMaster is mature with one mature Team and one stabilizing Team	ScrumMaster could start a third Team, but should be recruiting a new ScrumMaster to take over one or more of their Teams

Q: Since the ScrumMaster just facilitates the meetings, they can be part-time, right?

A: A part-time ScrumMaster can give a part-time effort to the role and perhaps even accomplish the basics. However, a full-time dedicated ScrumMaster can help the Team achieve previously unheard of levels of productivity. There is a great article by Michael James, CST that suggests ways in which a ScrumMaster can help their Team thrive (http://www.scrummasterchecklist.org).

Smells (Problems For the ScrumMaster Role)

Smell: The ScrumMaster has become nothing more than an administrative assistant for the Team (we call this the "Scrum Scribe").

Solution: The ScrumMaster should work to elevate their status in the Team's eyes. Practices like "You think it, you write it" will put administrative duties back on the Team and allow the ScrumMaster to re-engage at a higher level.

Smell: The ScrumMaster is a mini-dictator, always telling the Team what to do and when to do it.

Solution: Help the ScrumMaster to realize that their job is to support the Team becoming Self-Organizing and Self-Managing. The only way to accomplish this goal is for the ScrumMaster to step away from dictating and driving the Team. The role is one of facilitating!

Servant Leadership (How To Lead In An Agile Culture)

Many of us may be used to the "do it or else" management style called command-and-control. This style of management plays to our fears and leaves us with a bad taste in our mouth. We may be less familiar with Servant Leadership, a different management style where we willingly follow the leader to help accomplish a mission bigger than ourselves. Let's take a quick sidebar to explore Servant Leadership in more detail, as it is the default leadership style necessary to help Scrum succeed.

My favorite author on the subject of Servant Leadership is James Hunter. He has a great definition for what Servant Leadership means...

> *"Servant leadership is the skill of influencing people to enthusiastically work together towards goals for the common good, with character that inspires confidence."—James Hunter*

Let's deconstruct this definition and look at it piece-by-piece...

Skill—Great news for all of us, we don't have to be naturally born Servant Leaders. Servant Leadership is a skill that can be learned and acquired over years of practice.

Influence—There are two primary types of influence; power and authority. Power comes from many sources; perhaps we have legitimate power granted to us by the organization that we work for by our position/title or we have expert power because of our knowledge/background. Power is easy because it's fast and convenient. Unfortunately, power doesn't last and gets old quickly. How many times do you like to be told what to do?

Authority, on the other hand, is something we must earn by serving others. Most of us would do anything for our parents because they served us as a child and we respect them. That doesn't mean they didn't discipline us from time to time, but the sum total of our interactions left us feeling indebted to them for having our best interests at heart. Authority is enduring and given freely when it's deserved.

Enthusiasm—Do you work with motivated individuals who are charging the hill? Or, do you work with people who count the minutes until quitting time? How can we expect to have a great team if they are not enthusiastic?

Goals for the common good—One of the core values of Scrum is focus. We need to ask ourselves, "Are we focused on adding business value back to our Stakeholders? Will what we're doing really make a difference? Is it the right thing to do?" A Servant Leader presents a vision of what we are to accomplish that should align with the key goals of the Stakeholders and ultimately, the organization.

Character—What happens when you bring bad news to someone? Do they smile and react calmly or do they blow up in your face? When we cannot control our emotional response to stimulus (i.e. someone telling us bad news), we lack character. Working hard to become the calm in the storm is where we develop character. When we remain calm, others around us will remain peaceful and can again focus on the mission at hand.

Confidence—We all want to feel like we made the right decision of who to follow; that the person leading us is sure of the mission and will lead us down the right path no matter what. Servant Leaders are sure of themselves and of their mission and radiate this in a humble way to their followers.

It's not easy, or always necessary, to be a Servant Leader (sometimes we may need a little command-and-control when the wheels are coming off the bus), but it is something we can strive to become better at. Let those you work with know that you are trying to become a better Servant Leader and have them call you out anytime you exhibit command-and-control tendencies. In the end, you will be a much better leader and liked more by those around you.

Stakeholders

The Stakeholder community is diverse; everyone from executives who are funding the Product development effort to managers, line employees, even customers who will consume and use the Product that the Scrum Team produces.

Stakeholders take a more passive role in the development process. They are involved, but not committed the same way the Scrum Team is.

Stakeholders need to have a voice and see results. Failure to identify, manage, and please Stakeholders can lead to a Product failure.

Traits Of An Effective Stakeholder

Subject matter experts in their chosen field of work, they should know the domain of the Product better than the Scrum Team does.

Available to the Scrum Team to provide information and insights to help make the Product better. May be involved in Visioning, Product Road-Mapping, Release Planning, Product Backlog Seeding, Prioritization, and Sprint Review meetings.

Willing to receive and digest information that the Scrum Team provides on their progress.

Key Attitude

"The Product that the Scrum Team produces for me has value, I need to be involved in providing ideas and seeing the results. Please don't keep me in the dark and feed me misinformation. I would rather be a part of the development process and informed of how things are actually going, the good, the bad, and the ugly."—Stakeholder

How The Stakeholders Participate In The Sprint

During the Sprint, the Stakeholders may be consulted when the Team is gathering requirements or needing feedback on design decisions. Note that some people think the ownership of "how" to design the solution lies in the hands of the Team only. From personal experience, I have always benefited from sharing my ideas for mplementation with the Stakeholders to get feedback even before I developed he Product Backlog Item. The Product Owner can consult with the Stakeholders or strategic planning, Product Backlog Seeding workshops, and Prioritization meetings. Also, the Product Owner and ScrumMaster should communicate with he Stakeholders regarding Team status at regular intervals throughout the Sprint. At the end of the Sprint, during the Sprint Review, the Stakeholders will attend the demo in order to view the progress that the Team has made as well as to give their feedback on new ideas or areas of improvement in the Product.

Stakeholder Q & A

Q: Where do Stakeholders come from?
A: Stakeholders typically come from one of three camps:

Management—everyone from Executives to line managers

Subject matter experts—people who have worked in the Domain of the product for numerous years and are experts on the subject matter at hand

End user community—the people who will be consuming/utilizing the Product

Q: The Project Management Institutes' (PMI) view on Stakeholders differs from what you are presenting here, what gives?
A: According to PMI, the Scrum Team would also be considered a Stakeholder. Agile makes the distinction of classifying the Scrum Team as a separate entity.

Q: What about the Project Sponsor? Aren't they Stakeholders too?
A: The Project Sponsor is the Stakeholder responsible for financing the development effort; their voice carries a lot of weight. Agile doesn't specifically recognize this role, other than calling them a Stakeholder, but taking them for granted is a sure fire recipe for trouble.

Smells (Problems For the Stakeholder Role)

Smell: The Stakeholders are micromanaging the Team. They are showing up at all the Scrum meetings and are insisting that they be involved in all design decisions. The Team is getting frustrated and confused.

Solution: The ScrumMaster should meet with the Stakeholders and find out why they feel the need to work so closely with the Team. Perhaps the Product Owner isn't working closely enough with them and should start inviting them to Product Backlog Seeding workshops and prioritization meetings. Perhaps the Stakeholders don't realize the impact their behavior is having on the Team and they just need to be told the consequences of their actions.

Smell: The Stakeholders have stopped attending all Sprint Reviews and have adopted the attitude of "We will look at the Product when you are done developing". The Scrum Team fears their lack of involvement in the development process is going to lead to numerous changes down the road.

Solution: The Product Owner and the ScrumMaster should meet with the Stakeholders to find out why they have withdrawn. Perhaps the Sprint Review meetings have become too technical and they have lost interest. Perhaps the Stakeholders have a scheduling issue and need the Sprint Reviews at a more convenient time. Perhaps the Stakeholders simply don't realize the impact their absence is having on the Team. It should be emphasized to the Stakeholders that the strength of an Agile approach is having their input throughout the process.

ROLES IN SCRUM SUMMARY—WHERE WE HAVE BEEN

We saw how the Scrum Team is composed of three separate roles: Team, Product Owner, and ScrumMaster.

We learned about Servant Leadership and how it should be the default style of management in a Scrum environment.

We explored the role of the Stakeholders and how they interact with the Scrum Team.

We kicked dirt in the face of the critics and poked a little fun at our past with the Pig and the Chicken analogy.

Why All The Pigs And Chickens?

You have reached the most controversial section of the entire book. There is great debate about the use of the Pigs and Chickens metaphor in the Agile community. Some people are very opposed to its use. They feel it has cultural, human resource, or respect issues. While the terms can be abused and that abuse can cause problems, we at Braintrust feel the analogy still has value. Rather than sweep it under the rug, we have chosen to poke a little fun at it and our past. So, without further ado, here is the story of the Pigs and the Chickens.

A pig and a chicken are planning to open a restaurant together. What to call it is the million dollar question. The chicken likes "Ham and Eggs", but the pig has his concerns...

Committed

In Scrum, we like to talk about the Scrum Team (Team Members, Product Owner, and ScrumMaster) as Pigs being committed to the Product development effort. The Scrum Team is in the trenches every day, making it happen. They are fully committed to the outcome of their effort (they have "skin in the game").

Involved

On the other hand, the Chickens (Stakeholders) are only involved in the Product development effort. Stakeholders' input is requested for strategic planning purposes during Product development, as needed, and during the Sprint reviews. Since the Stakeholders are not in the trenches every day (like the Scrum Team) we consider them to only be involved.

A Word of Caution

In the past, people have abused the notion of Pigs and Chickens. Teams have been known to ostracize and isolate Stakeholders from their meetings - even going as far as belittling Stakeholders with comments such as "You are a Chicken. You are not allowed to speak." Please remember that any development effort is a partnership. The role of the Chickens is no less than the Pigs; it's just different. By recognizing this fact and treating Stakeholders with respect, we all can be more successful.

MEETINGS (CEREMONIES) IN SCRUM

WHAT'S AHEAD IN THIS SECTION

Ready, set, Sprint!

The key meetings in Scrum

Sprint Planning

Daily Scrum

Product Backlog Refinement

Sprint Review

Sprint Retrospective

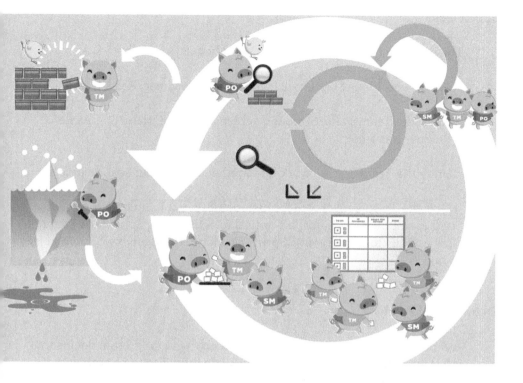

he Sprint is a **Timeboxed** period of work at the end of which the Team delivers
Potentially Shippable Product Increment. Originally designed to be 30 days to
t the calendar month, in practice, Teams have adopted Sprint lengths anywhere
etween 2 to 4 weeks. We have even seen several Teams with one week Sprints. All
prints should have a Sprint Goal, a unifying theme helping people understand
hat is to be accomplished in the Sprint. The Sprint Goal oftentimes flows directly
om the Product Roadmap/Release Plan. Each Sprint is fixed-scope, with the Team
gning up for as much work as they feel they can comfortably complete within the
me frame of the sprint. The Team will take each placeholder for a requirement
Product Backlog Item) and develop it until it reaches a "Done" state (Production
eady). At the end of the Sprint, the new feature(s) completed are considered
otentially Shippable, meaning the Product Owner can now make the decision to
ut them into Production usage if they see the Business Value in doing so.

Sprint Goal

The unifying theme or goal of the Sprint helps:

Tie the work of the Sprint back to the Product Roadmap/Release Plan

Focus the Team's efforts around achieving a Potentially Shippable Product Increment

Unify the Team around working together, rather than as individuals

Give the Team some room for negotiability in its implementation of the Sprint Backlog Items. It's critical to achieve the Sprint Goal, but not necessarily to implement a Sprint Backlog Item in an exact and precise way.

Definition of Ready

A Product Backlog Item is considered **Ready** when the Team deems that it has been sufficiently refined to a small enough size to be completed within a single Sprint. It's important for the Team not to commit to completing any Product Backlog Items that do not meet the Team's definition of Ready or they may invite failure into the Sprint. Prior to starting their Sprint, it's important for a Scrum Team to create a common definition of Ready, so everyone is on the same page.

Definition of Done

Similar to the Definition of Ready it is important for the entire Scrum Team to be on the same page about the definition of Done. A **Definition of Done** should include a of the Tasks the Scrum Team deems necessary to build a quality Product Increment which may include quality assurance and quality control Tasks. A common Definition of Done should be agreed upon prior to the Scrum Team starting the Sprint where it can be influenced by organizational standards that may impact the development process. Meeting Acceptance Criteria can be an important part of the Team's Definition of Done, but is typically only a subset of the Tasks necessary to create a quality Product Increment. Having a common Definition of Done prevents surprises (but you said it was "Done"!) and helps eliminate Technical Debt.

Quick Take

Who Attends: The Scrum Team

Duration: Depends on the length of the Sprint. It is recommended that no more than 2 hours per week of Sprint be spent in Sprint Planning (E.g. for a 2 week Sprint, this meeting is capped at 4 hours).

Location: Somewhere convenient for the Scrum Team

Frequency: It's the kickoff meeting of each and every Sprint. The new Sprint begins when the Scrum Team enters the room for Sprint Planning.

Purpose: To determine the Sprint Goal and the work that the Team commits to accomplish during the Sprint

Overview

In Sprint Planning, the work for the Sprint is determined. Generally there are 2 separate conversations in this meeting, each of which is typically 1/2 the duration of the total meeting time. The first conversation, attended by the entire Scrum Team, is where items from the Product Backlog deemed Ready are selected for inclusion in the Sprint. We call this the "What" conversation. Then, the Team meets for the "How" conversation to finalize the Sprint Backlog, decomposing the selected Product Backlog Items into Tasks and estimating each Task in Ideal Hours. The "How" conversation is technical in nature and doesn't require the Product Owner's full attention.

The **Sprint Planning** meeting is just that - the meeting where the Goals and objectives of the Sprint are planned. The Team Members, Product Owner, and ScrumMaster attend this meeting. The key objective is to define the Sprint Goal and pull items from the Product Backlog and add them to the Sprint Backlog. This meeting is held once each Sprint, and signals the beginning of the Sprint. The mos important feature of this meeting is that the Team chooses the items that go into the Sprint Backlog. The Product Owner will provide the Team with highest busines priorities, but the Team decides what work will be accomplished during the Sprint.

Suggested Meeting Agenda

The "What" conversation, Part 1 (½ the Timebox)

Call to order

Product Owner reviews

Product Vision

Product Roadmap

Product Release Plan

Highest Priority Backlog Items with the Team (Note: Only review Product Backlog Items meeting the Definition of Ready)

The Team and the ScrumMaster review

Technical Debt

Velocity/Capacity for the Sprint (Be sure to note anyone with a planned absence or distraction)

Outcome (I.e. Action items) from the last Sprint Retrospective

The Product Owner and Team craft a Sprint Goal and agree on the scope for the Sprint (I.e. how many Backlog Items the Team feels comfortable completing this Sprint).

Take a bio/coffee break

The "How" conversation, Part 2 (1/2 the Timebox)

The Team decomposes the Product Backlog Items in the Sprint Backlog into Tasks.

> While the Product Owner isn't a key member of this discussion, it is good to have them accessible in case any questions come up.

> The Team may need to complete some high-level design in order to complete this step.

The Team estimates each Task in Ideal Hours

The Team and the ScrumMaster verify the summation of hours on all Tasks does not exceed the Teams total **Capacity**.

The ScrumMaster checks with the Team to make sure they are still comfortable with the Commitment they have made.

> If the Team is over-Committed, the Product Owner is needed to de-scope some Product Backlog Item(s) from the Sprint.

> If the Team is under-Committed, the Product Owner is needed to present some additional Product Backlog Items for inclusion in the Sprint.

The Team agrees that the commitment to the Sprint Goal is doable and the Sprint Backlog is fixed.

Adjourn

Sprint Planning Meeting Q & A

Q: If this is a Planning meeting, why are no Stakeholders invited?
A: In Scrum, the Product Owner represents the voice of the Stakeholders. The Sprint is very tactical in nature and therefore too low level to the Stakeholders to be involved in deeply. Think about going to a restaurant. You place your order with the waiter then wait patiently for your delicious meal. How many times do you go back to the kitchen to plan the cooking and check on its progress? Never, for most of us. The same level of trust should apply in this case; we trust the Product Owner (waiter) and the Team (the kitchen staff) to deliver what was ordered.

Q: What is Velocity and why does it factor into this meeting?
A: Velocity is a historical measure of how much work the Team can complete in a Sprint. There are 2 main ways to calculate Velocity; first is **Yesterday's Weather**, which is using the Velocity from the last Sprint and second is taking a rolling

average of the last 3 Sprints (a rolling average is more accurate than averaging all Sprints, because things change quickly in an Agile environment). Velocity is typically measured in Story Points (a form of Relative Estimation that compares the complexity of one Product Backlog Item to another). Once a Team's Velocity is known, they can use the number in the Sprint Planning "What" conversation to figure out how many Story Points worth of Product Backlog Items to commit to.

Q: You speak of the "What" and "How" conversation as if they are 2 separate meetings. We do ours at the same time. Is that ok?
A: Some Teams elect to comingle the "What" and "How" conversations, flowing from one to the other as needed. The reason to separate them is out of respect for the Product Owner. If the Product Owner is not technical, the "How" conversation will be over their head and of little interest to them. If your Product Owner doesn't mind staying the entire time, there is nothing wrong with either way of holding the meeting.

Q: The ScrumMaster is responsible for assigning the Tasks to the individual Team Members during the Sprint Planning "How" conversation, correct?
A: The Sprint Backlog (committed to Product Backlog Items and the Tasks to get them done) is a "pull-system" of work. By leaving all the Tasks unassigned during the Sprint, a Team Member can pull the next Task that appeals to them should they need more work. This "pull-system" promotes intrinsic (something you choose to do) versus extrinsic (something forced upon you) motivation, critical to the success of Agile.

Q: Sure seems like a long time for a meeting. Why is that?
A: Abe Lincoln once said that if he had six hours to chop down a tree, he would spend the first four sharpening his axe. There is simply no substitute for great preparation. By laying out what will happen during the Sprint before it ever begins, the Team operates almost as if by script. Everything is carefully orchestrated.

Smells (Problems For the Sprint Planning Meeting)

Smell: The Sprint Planning meeting is taking a lot longer than you suggest. Why is that?

Solution: The typical cause of this problem is that the Product Backlog is in rough shape. The Product Backlog Items are probably too high-level and have lots of hidden scope. When the Team starts thinking of the "How", they are overwhelmed and start asking lots of questions, leading to even more discovery. By implementing a process called Product Backlog Refinement (working one to two Sprints ahead on refining Product Backlog Items and the top of the Product Backlog), everyone can be better prepared going into Sprint Planning and accomplish the true intent of the meeting.

Smell: Our Product Owner doesn't want to be involved in Sprint Planning. They claim they don't have time to attend and the Product Backlog is already prioritized so the Team should just pick the Product Backlog Items they are comfortable completing.

Solution: Like most of the meetings in Scrum, the value is in the conversation. Without having the Product Owner in the discussion, the conversation becomes one-sided and the Team can easily lose valuable feedback necessary for their success. If this is happening to you, the ScrumMaster should step in and counsel the Product Owner about the need to have them attend. If the Product Owner still doesn't attend, then the ScrumMaster should escalate the Team's concern to management.

Smell: The Team is getting way too technical in the Sprint Planning Meeting. In fact, they sometimes start working on the Product Backlog Items in the meeting itself.

Solution: The Team is technical and they live and breathe details. It is not uncommon for them to want to get detailed and start solving problems. If this is happening, the ScrumMaster should step in and remind the Team of the intent and purpose of the meeting. The ScrumMaster should try to elevate the discussion and get the Team back on track with the true intent of the Sprint Planning Meeting, planning the Sprint.

Smell: Our Team comes into the Sprint Planning meeting without Sizes placed on the Product Backlog Items and we Size during this meeting. This seems too late to me, but I am not sure. Any advice?

Solution: It is our recommendation that you Size your entire Product Backlog as soon as possible then perform maintenance Sizing along the way. Having the entire Product Backlog Sized allows the Product Owner to be more informed when planning releases (Release Planning), tracking progress (creating a Burn-Up Chart), and Prioritizing.

Daily Scrum (Daily Standup)

Who Attends: The Scrum Team (Team, Product Owner, and ScrumMaster)

Duration: No more than 15 minutes

Location: Somewhere convenient for the Team (preferably in front of the Team's Scrum Board)

Frequency: Every workday

Purpose: To synchronize the Teams efforts at meeting the Sprint Goal by sharing progress, making commitments, and asking for help

Overview

The **Daily Scrum** meeting, often nicknamed The Daily Stand-Up (more on why later), is the most tactical of all the Scrum meetings. This meeting is held each workday during the Sprint. A popular question often asked is, "What time of day should the Daily Scrum be held?" The best answer is a question, "What time of day can the Scrum Team consistently commit to coming together for 15 uninterrupted minutes?"

Purpose ("Why")

Like it or not, the longer individuals go without touching base, the more likely hey are to lose focus and procrastinate. Sprints are short (2 to 4 weeks generally) and there isn't a lot of time to recover if Tasks have slipped off the front burner. By coming together each day, we are being held accountable in front of our peers. This is a powerful form of social pressure aiding in motivation to make continual progress. In addition, by being allowed to discuss Roadblocks on a daily basis, we are encouraged to ask for help in a public forum. When a problem is brought up in a group setting, more people hear about it and you have a greater chance of finding a solution faster. Also, Roadblocks can commonly occur to different Team Members working on similar tasks. By holding the meeting daily, the opportunity for procrastination shrinks and we can move from being reactive to being proactive. In summary, this meeting is intended to be a time for the Scrum Team to connect, refocus, discuss current progress, and ask for help. The meeting establishes a daily pulse (often called cadence) for the Scrum Team.

Suggested Meeting Agenda

Call to order

Answering the 3 questions (Each person answers all 3 questions before proceeding to the next person.)

What did I do yesterday to help move the Sprint Goal to completion (Or today, depending on when the meeting is held)?

What am I going to do today to help move the Sprint Goal to completion (Or tomorrow, depending on when the meeting is held)?

What are your roadblocks (Often shortened to simply "blockers")?

Review the Team's Burn-Down Chart

Adjourn

Daily Scrum Meeting Q & A

: What is the ScrumMaster's role in The Daily Scrum?
: The ScrumMaster attends in order to understand how he or she can help clear Roadblocks for the Team. Team members are encouraged to work through their own Roadblocks first, but ScrumMaster assistance may be necessary. The ScrumMaster can report on the progress at clearing Roadblocks, helping provide greater accountability and transparency to the Team. We caution ScrumMasters not to lead by asking the 3 questions, simply to listen for Roadblocks and let the Team own the meeting.

Q: Why does the Product Owner attend the meeting? Someone told me they were a Chicken and can attend, but shouldn't be allowed to speak.
A: The Product Owner is a pig and an integral part of the Scrum Team. Without their daily involvement, the Team may not have critical information they need for success. Having the Product Owner in the Daily Scrum allows them to be informed of the Team's progress as well as challenges. The Product Owner may also be needed to help clear Roadblocks on occasion.

Q: Why is the meeting nicknamed The Daily Stand-Up?
A: By standing, the intent is to keep the meeting short and to the point. Attendees do not have a chance to sit and get too comfortable, which could lead to a longer meeting.

Smells (Problems For the Daily Scrum)

Smell: One or more Scrum Team members are habitually late or skipping the meeting altogether.

Solution: Meet with the individual(s) in private and discuss the reasons for their tardiness/absence. Let them know how they are impacting the Team and come-up with suggestions for changing their behavior.

Smell: The meeting lasts longer than 15 minutes.

Solution: Assuming your Team is the prescribed size (7 +/- 2 - If it's not, the Team size is the first issue to address), you may be trying to solve issues in this meeting. Note issues as Roadblocks and IDS (identify, discuss, solve) them directly after the meeting.

Smell: The Stakeholders insist on attending the meeting and they are very disruptive (they ask questions or jump in adding their two cents).

Solution: Meet with the Stakeholder(s) and do a root cause analysis. Is there a particular reason they are compelled to attend and disrupt the meeting. Try the 5 Why's technique (keeping asking "Why" five times in a row, thinking like a 2 year old) to get to the root cause. More often than not, the Stakeholder has a current need for additional communication not being met by the Product Owner and ScrumMaster.

Product Backlog Refinement

Quick Take

Who Attends: The Scrum Team (Team, Product Owner, and ScrumMaster)

Duration: 5 to 10% of the total Sprint duration

Location: Somewhere convenient for the Team (preferably in front of the Team's Scrum Board)

Frequency: As agreed upon by the Scrum Team

Purpose: To prepare the near term Product Backlog Items for implementation in future Sprints

Overview

The core focus of the Sprint is to deliver Potentially Shippable Product Increments. These increments are made up of one or more Product Backlog Items. One of the keys to success in Scrum is being able to take a Product Backlog Item into a Sprint and get it to a "Done" state. Unfortunately, many Product Backlog Items are large and therefore contain a lot of hidden scope. When the Team commits to completing a large Product Backlog Item, they typically don't have time to get it done and fail their Sprint. Product Backlog Refinement is a time for the Team to meet with the Product Owner to familiarize themself with the Product Backlog Items about to be implemented. Once the Team is familiar with the Product Backlog Item, they can decompose it into smaller Product Backlog Items if deemed necessary. This way, the Team is familiar with highest Priority Product Backlog Items before committing to implementing them in Sprint Planning.

Purpose ("Why")

Product Backlog Refinement is the newest meeting added to the Scrum process. The need for the meeting came from the community. Teams quickly learned that if they go into the Sprint unprepared, they often end up missing the mark when trying to implement Product Backlog Items. They may not fully understand the needs of the Stakeholders and implement the wrong solution. Or worse yet, they don't realize how large a Product Backlog Item is and simply cannot complete it on time. Product Backlog Refinement was therefore added to give the Team and the Product Owner time to do their homework so they can better prepare for the up-coming Sprint.

Suggested Meeting Agenda

Call to order

Cycle through as many Product Backlog Items as necessary until the Timebox expires

>   Product Owner Reviews a Product Backlog Item with the Team

>   The Team asks questions and the Product Owner clarifies (Note: If the Product Owner can't answer the Team's question, the Product Owner takes a homework assignment to get the answer)

>   The Team and Product Owner decompose the Product Backlog Item into one or more smaller Product Backlog Items.

>   Each new Product Backlog Item is Sized and Acceptance Criteria is created/updated

Adjourn

Product Backlog Q & A

Q: The Team says that the Product Backlog Item is large and there is no way to break it into smaller Product Backlog Items.
A: This appears to be more of a mental block than anything else. Anything can be broken down into smaller parts with the right motivation. The ScrumMaster should challenge the Team's thinking and push them to think "outside the box" and innovate

Q: Do I really need the entire Team in the room for Product Backlog Refinement? That is a lot of people and seems like a waste.

A: First off, we should remember that Scrum is a Team sport. Having the entire Team in the room helps to foster **High Bandwidth** communication, which gets everyone on the same page. In addition to adding Team synchronization, everyone is able to lend their expertise when it comes to decomposing the Product Backlog items being refined and brainstorm possible solutions to their implementation.

Smells (Problems For the Product Backlog Refinement)

Smell: Despite our best efforts, the Team wants to get very technical in this meeting. They get so wrapped up in the details of implementing the Product Backlog Item, they start to lose focus on the actual goal of the meeting.

Solution: Teams by their very nature want to implement Product Backlog Items. It's very natural for them to want to jump in and start solving the problem. When the Team is getting too detailed, it's time for the ScrumMaster to step-in and remind them of the mission of the meeting, effectively pulling them up out of the weeds.

Smell: We meet for Product Backlog Refinement however, our Product Owner seems to review Product Backlog Items at random or even lets the Team choose which ones need refinement. It feels like there is no clear priority and we refine the wrong Product Backlog Items.

Solution: We want our Product Backlog Refinement meetings to be focused. There is no sense refining low Priority Product Backlog Items because they many never make it into a Sprint for implementation. The ScrumMaster should work with the Product Owner to ensure they understand how to Prioritize their Product Backlog and are only bringing high-Priority Product Backlog Items into the Product Backlog Refinement meeting.

The Sprint Review Meeting

Quick Take

Who Attends: All interested parties: Stakeholders, Team Members, Product Owner and ScrumMaster

Duration: Depends on the length of the Sprint. It is recommended that no more than one hour per week of Sprint be spent in Reviewing. For a 2 week Sprint, the meeting is capped at two hours.

Location: Somewhere that allows for a Product demonstration and convenience of all attendees

Frequency: Once per Sprint

Purpose: To demonstrate and seek feedback on the work accomplished during the current Sprint

Overview

At the end of the Sprint, the Team will have a Potentially Shippable Product Increment. The Product Increment is made up of all the Product Backlog Items the Product Owner agrees meet the Team's Definition of Done. In the Sprint Review, the Chickens (Stakeholders) get to see what was accomplished, hear what work was accepted or rejected, and provide feedback and new ideas.

Purpose ("Why")

The Sprint review meeting is the culmination of the work accomplished during the Sprint. It is like a show and tell session (some Teams call it "The Showcase" for this reason). Here, the Team gets to show off the fruits of their labor from the current Sprint. In this meeting, the Team has the opportunity to demonstrate the solutions developed during the Sprint. The Sprint Review meeting is held on the last day of the Sprint when the Sprint backlog is exhausted. As part of this meeting, all attendees provide input and feedback on the solution being demonstrated. From this meeting, more items may be added to the Product Backlog and requirements can potentially change. At the core of this meeting is the Empirical Process, our primary opportunity to Inspect and Adapt the Product.

Suggested Meeting Agenda

Call to order

Product Owner reviews:

> Product Vision

> Product Roadmap

> Product Release Plan

> The Sprint Backlog

Team gives a Demo of the Potentially Shippable Product Increment

Product Owner formally accepts or rejects each Product Backlog Item in the Sprint Backlog

Everyone brainstorms new ideas and documents them as new Product Backlog Items

Product Owner reviews what is coming up next and seeks feedback from the Stakeholders

Adjourn

Sprint Review Meeting Q & A

Q: This meeting seems a bit long. Why is that?
A: The Sprint Review meeting is so much more than a Product Demo. It is also an opportunity for the Team to "show off", which is extremely important in building morale. It is one of the most important chances for them to hear directly from their Stakeholders and get that crucial feedback to improve the Product. It is also an opportunity for everyone to agree on what's next for the Team to develop.

Q: What happens if the Demo doesn't go so well?
A: The Sprint Review continues as planned. Any features that do not pass the Sprint Review are added back to the Product Backlog then reprioritized along with any other remaining work. A common reason that a Product Backlog Item may be rejected is because it contains Technical Debt and therefore doesn't meet the Scrum Team's Definition of Done.

Q: How can I get my Stakeholders to spend this much time in one meeting?
A: That is the job of the Product Owner. In their role, they are constantly interacting with and getting buy-in from the Stakeholders. By delivering consistently and keeping the Sprint Review meeting interesting and engaging, this will be one meeting everyone looks forward to at the end of each Sprint.

Smells (Problems For the Sprint Review Meeting)

Smell: The ScrumMaster insists on leading the Demo during the Sprint Review.

Solution: Time for an intervention! Either the Team or the Product Owner should confront the ScrumMaster and let them know that it is demoralizing to the Team for them to lead the Demo. Since the ScrumMaster isn't doing the work, why should they get all the credit for the Team's accomplishments? It is preferred that the Product Owner lead the meeting and allow the Team to do the demo, although it is acceptable for the Product Owner to lead the demo too.

Smell: I didn't realize Stakeholders were invited to this meeting? We usually only do the Demo for our Product Owner. It's their first time seeing what we have done and we don't want to embarrass them in front of the Stakeholders.

Solution: A good Product Owner is going to spend time with the Team reviewing completed Product Backlog Items along the way as they are developed. By the time the Sprint Review happens, they should have seen multiple Demos of the Potentially Shippable Product Increment. The purpose of the Sprint Review meeting is for everyone (especially the

Stakeholders) to Inspect and Adapt the Potentially Shippable Product Increment.

Smell: We invite our Stakeholders to our Sprint Review, but they never show up. Later they tell us they don't like what we have developed and we have to do it all over again.

Solution: It is critical to have as many Stakeholders as possible at your Sprint Review meeting. Have your Product Owner do a root cause analysis with the Stakeholders as to why they are not attending. Is the meeting at an inconvenient time? Move it. Do the Stakeholders not see value in attending? Change the agenda to make it more valuable.

Smell: Our Stakeholders attend, but never provide feedback.

Solution: It is not uncommon for the Stakeholders to watch the Demo, clap their hands, say "Nice job", and leave. It is up to The Scrum Team to invite/welcome feedback from the Stakeholders when this occurs. One tip is to give each Stakeholder some index cards and markers at the start of the meeting and request that they write down at least one new idea before the meeting ends.

Smell: Our Product Owner only shows up for our Sprint Planning and Sprint Review meetings. They are virtually impossible to find during our Sprint. Therefore, every Sprint Review, they seem shocked at what we have developed and they never like it. This is very frustrating because it negatively affects our Velocity and we feel like we are always back-tracking. We came up with a clever solution to this problem and have created extensive Acceptance Criteria for each Product Backlog Item. If the Product Owner refuses to agree to the Acceptance Criteria in Sprint Planning, then we refuse to accept the Product Backlog Item into the Sprint Backlog. Please help, this seems a bit too confrontational!

Solution: Typically, when the Product Owner habitually doesn't sign off on the Team's work, it's a symptom of an absentee Product Owner. The Team should engage the Product Owner more in the development process and ask for their sign-off before the Sprint Review meeting. This will prevent the Product Owner from being surprised during the Demo and lead to them being more in line with the Team.

Quick Take

Who Attends: The Scrum Team

Duration: Depends on the length of the Sprint. It is recommended that no more than 45 minutes per week of Sprint be spent in the Retrospective. For a 2 week Sprint, this meeting is capped at 1.5 hours.

Location: Somewhere convenient for the Scrum Team

Frequency: Once per Sprint

Purpose: To review what went right, what was challenging, and the opportunities for improvement from the current Sprint

Overview

At the completion of each Sprint, the Retrospective meeting is held. This intimate gathering of the Scrum Team is unique in that no Product Development work takes place. This is when the Scrum Team gets better—through inspection and adaptation. The Team evaluates how they can perform even better for the next Sprint. This meeting benefits the Scrum Team directly, which ultimately benefits the Product and Stakeholders as a whole.

Purpose ("Why")

All processes benefit from a "Lessons Learned" session. For Scrum, this is that meeting. The Sprint Retrospective is the last meeting held to wrap up the Sprint. Its purpose is to give the Scrum Team an opportunity to uncover and share lessons arned. They discuss what worked well and what could be improved upon from a print perspective. In other words, the Retrospective meeting improves upon the rocess of the Sprint itself and not the Product under construction. Some people ull Scrum a continuous improvement framework, and this meeting is one of the rimary reasons it got that label.

Suggested Meeting Agenda

Call to order

Set the stage

Gather data

Look for patterns and assign priority

Create an action plan

Adjourn

 ## Sprint Retrospective Meeting Q & A

: Why is this meeting limited to just the Team?
: By only involving the Team, they are more likely to be open and forthcoming ith ideas for improvement. Having the Stakeholders in the room may cause social 'essure to embellish the truth and hide the details.

: How does the Team know which improvements to focus on?
: This process becomes easier for each Sprint. Ideally, the ideas for improvement e observable, quantifiable, and measurable. They should also be ones the Team in directly control. By measuring and tracking, the Team learns quickly how fective their Retrospective meetings are.

: So why not hold this meeting before the Sprint Review?
: By keeping the Sprint Retrospective after the Sprint Review, the Team has an portunity to discuss how to improve the Review meeting as well. Also, the lessons arned for the Team have nothing to do with the Product itself; those should relate ily to the work processes and interactions within the Team. This is not something be discussed with the Chickens (Stakeholders) in the room.

Smell: One Team member is very vocal and won't let the other Team members talk during the meeting. This individual's personality is so strong, they border on being abusive to the others. Everyone is getting frustrated, but not willing to say anything out of fear of retribution.

Solution: In this case, it's up to the ScrumMaster to privately confront the Team Member who is too vocal and let them know what is going on. It's important to describe the specific behavior and not attack the individual personally. A praise sandwich is sometimes a good way to address behaviors one wants to change. A praise sandwich starts with praising an individual about something they do well, then mention their inappropriate behavior and follow-up with praise about another good thing they do. If this doesn't work, it may be necessary to get Human Resources (HR) involved to work with the individual.

Smell: The Sprint Retrospectives have gotten stale. The Scrum Team seems to reach the same conclusions over-and-over again. In fact, they are thinking (or already have) of shortening the meeting to only 30 minutes to get it over with faster.

Solution: It is up to the ScrumMaster to keep the Sprint Retrospectives fresh and interesting. There are a number of ways to add new life to them; move locations, change the facilitator, come up with a new agenda for the meeting. By always varying one or more elements of the meeting, they will feel fresh and exciting.

Smell: We love the idea behind the Sprint Retrospective, but it doesn't seem to work. We always agree that we need to improve something like "communication" but in the next Sprint Retrospective we always say the same thing. Nothing ever seems to change. I feel like we are stuck in an endless loop. Help!

Solution: Before concluding the Sprint Retrospective it is important to leave with a very clear list of Tasks (and owners of those tasks) in order to make effective change. To say that "communication" needs to improve, isn't really saying anything SMART (i.e. Specific, Measurable, Actionable, Realistic, and Timely). Try being more specific and see what happens next time.

We saw how a Sprint is typically a two to four week period of time and at the end of which the Team is delivering a Potentially Shippable Product Increment.

We defined some common terms like:

Sprint Goal

Definition of Ready

Definition of Done

We learned that every Sprint begins with a "what" and "how" conversation during Sprint Planning.

We learned about the heartbeat of the Sprint with the Daily Scrum.

We saw the importance of devoting time during the Sprint to focus on refining the Product Backlog.

We stood in awe of the wonderful inspect and adapt loop built into Scrum with the Sprint Review and the Sprint Retrospective.

ARTIFACTS IN SCRUM

WHAT'S AHEAD IN THIS SECTION

Artifacts are all the things left behind in our wake. Scrum is pretty silent when it comes to what to document. It leaves most of the decisions up to you, your Team, and your organization. At a minimum, we want you to consider the following:

Core Scrum Artifacts

    Product Backlog

    Sprint Backlog

    Product Increment

Additional Scrum Artifacts

    Velocity

    Burn-Up Chart

    Burn-Down Chart

    Scrum Board

Product Backlog

Definition and Usage

Fundamentally, the Product Backlog is a list of all the work needing to be accomplished across all Sprints. It is typically made of up new features, change requests, and any defects discovered in the Product. Everyone contributes to the Product Backlog Items in the Product Backlog; Stakeholders and Scrum Team Members. The Product Owner is responsible for owning, maintaining/refining, and prioritizing the Product Backlog. It is essential for the Product Backlog to contain only items which have a chance of being implemented (i.e. has business value), so that no time or effort is wasted.

Context

The Product Backlog exists independent of the Sprints.

Setup

Comes from everyone; Product Owners go out into the wild to collect Product Backlog Items from the Stakeholder and the Scrum Team

Often documented as User Stories (i.e. As a..., I want..., so that...)

> E.g. As a swimmer, I want a salt water filtration system, so that my hair doesn't turn green

Should have Acceptance Criteria; a few statements of what it means to be done from a business point of view

> E.g. Verify that after swimming my hair isn't green

The Product Backlog needs to be Prioritized. Several factors need to be consider when determining Priority:

> Business Value—A measure of ROI (can be objective or subjective) to the business

> Complexity—A **Relative Estimate** generated by the Team

> Whatever else makes sense for your environment (e.g. Exciter, Regulation, Risk, etc.)

The Product Owner: While the Product Owner is responsible for maintaining the Product Backlog, it is important to involve a good number of Stakeholders, Team Members, and the ScrumMaster in writing Product Backlog Items. A good Product Owner will seek Product Backlog Items from everyone.

Smells (Problems For the Product Backlog)

Smell 1: Prioritizing the Product Backlog in a vacuum (i.e. Product Owner doesn't seek Stakeholder, Team, and/or ScrumMaster feedback) can lead to trouble. Everyone wants to know that they have a voice and it has been heard. When the Product Owner doesn't take other's feedback into account, they may find Stakeholders or Team Members plotting against them. It's best for the Product Owner to involve many people in Prioritizing the Product Backlog.

Smell 2: The Product Backlog is not meant to replace more detailed requirements gathering. It is meant to be a place holder for it. Avoid getting too detailed with the individual Product Backlog Items. Remember, in Agile/Scrum, we only want to get detailed at the last responsible moment, right before the Team goes to implement a Product Backlog Item during the Sprint. That means in the Sprint, as the Team is a about to implement the Product Backlog Item, they should consult with the Product Owner and/or Stakeholders on the specifics of what they are about to create.

Smell 3: On the other side of the coin, if the Product Backlog Items are left too broad (some people call these *Epics*), there may be too much scope and the Team may struggle to complete them in a single Sprint. The trick is to strike a balance and continually refine the Product Backlog Items that are close to being implemented so that they are small enough to fit in Sprints, but not too small that they end up becoming full requirements.

Sprint Backlog

Definition and Usage

The Sprint Backlog is the collection of Product Backlog Items and the Tasks necessary to accomplish them that the Team has committed to delivering at the end of the Sprint. A new Sprint Backlog is determined at the beginning of every Sprint during the Sprint Planning meeting. The Team owns the Sprint Backlog and is responsible for getting it Done prior to the end of the Sprint.

Context

The Sprint

Setup

During Sprint Planning the following items are determined

> "What"—Which Product Backlog Items will be included in the Sprint Backlog
> "How"—The Tasks necessary to accomplish the selected Product Backlog Items

Responsible Party

The Team

Smells (Problems For the Sprint Backlog)

Smell 1: From time-to-time the Team may create large Tasks (tasks taking more than 2 days to complete). Large Tasks are dangerous in Scrum because they are not very Transparent and have a tendency to grow in size.

Smell 2: Over committing by putting too many Product Backlog Items in the Sprint Backlog is a common problem among Teams today. Knowing your Team's Velocity and being conservative are your keys to a successful Sprint.

Product Increment

Definition and Usage

There is a joke in the Agile community... "When is a Product done? After the very first Iteration." While most Stakeholders don't think this joke is funny, it does serve a purpose. After each and every Sprint, the Scrum Team is releasing another Potentially Shippable Product Increment. It then becomes a business decision about whether or not to start using this new functionality.

The **Product Increment** is the collection of all the completed Product Backlog

Items that start accumulating after the very first Sprint. Since we have focused on building the highest business value features first, the early Product Increments should be quite useful and valuable to the business.

Context

The Product

Setup

The output of every Sprint is a Potentially Shippable Product Increment

Responsible Party

The Scrum Team

Smell 1: A Product Owner who isn't truly on the same page with their stakeholders may have the Team building a Product Increment that no one will use or find value in. It's very important that the Product Owner align the needs of the business to the Product Increment so that this situation can be avoided.

Smell 2: If too much Technical Debt is allowed to accumulate, the integrity of the Product Increment may be compromised, rendering it ineffective. Technical Debt is a fact of life and it must be paid off early and often. By adding Technical Debt to our Product Backlog, scheduling it into Sprints, and releasing solutions into the Product Increment, we can ensure a stable and useable Product Increment.

Smell 3: Some Scrum Teams make the mistake of not including Integration when they setup their Definition of Done. If the newly completed Product Backlog Items don't work with the existing Product Backlog Items, the Product Increment is not complete. Integrate early and often to avoid incurring Integration Technical Debt.

ADDITIONAL ARTIFACTS RECOMMENDED FOR SCRUM

While not considered core Scrum artifacts, most Scrum Teams find the addition of the following artifacts to be of tremendous value.

Velocity

Definition and Usage

Velocity is a measure of how much work is completed by the Team in a Sprint. A simple way to calculate Velocity is to count the number of Product Backlog Items accepted by the Product Owner at the Sprint Review meeting.

By knowing the Team's Velocity, a number of benefits can be gained:

Velocity becomes a great predictor for Release and Sprint Planning.

By knowing the Team's Velocity, the Product Owner can better manage Stakeholder expectations in terms of Team output and Capacity planning.

Teams can use velocity to understand their level of performance and challenge themselves to increase their performance level over time.

Context

The entire Product Development effort for one Scrum Team

Setup

In order for a Velocity to be established, one or more Sprints must be executed.

There are two popular techniques for estimating a Scrum Team's Velocity:

Yesterday's Weather—The Scrum Team uses the Velocity of the last Sprint in order to plan the current one

Rolling average of the last three Sprints

Responsible Party

The Team and ScrumMaster

Smells (Problems For Velocity)

Smell 1: In the absence of traditional metrics, Stakeholders may start using Velocity as the primary measure of a Team's success. They may even start to compare two or more Scrum Team's by their Velocity. Velocity is a "Team thing" and specific to each individual Scrum Team therefore, not comparable across Teams. Also, when used as the primary measure of a Team's progress, the Team ma revolt and start gaming Velocity. It's easy to shrink Product Backlog Items to show an inflated Velocity when the Team feels cornered.

Smell 2: It is unreasonable for the Product Owner and the Stakeholders to expect the Team's Velocity to never fluctuate. Murphy's Law (whatever can go wrong, will), vacations, holidays, and unplanned sick leave can all cause a tempora drop in Velocity. Remind everyone to look at the big picture and not get caught up random occurrence.

Smell 3: Plotting Velocity, Sprint over Sprint, can be a great way to look for trends of either high or declining performance. By taking time to review the Team Velocity, perhaps during the Sprint Retrospective, problems can be detected and addressed early before getting out of hand.

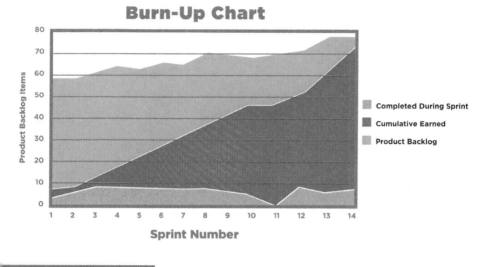

The **Burn-Up Chart** is a graphical depiction of the total size of the Product Backlog as well as how much of the Product Backlog has been completed. Favored by the Product Owner for its macro view of the Product development effort, it is a very popular tool. The Product Owner can use the Burn-Up Chart to predict future delivery dates and communicate Team progress to the Stakeholders. Because the use of the Burn-Up Chart depicts the entire Product Development effort, progress is generally plotted at the completion of each Sprint. In this manner, work is not credited towards the overall Product's progress until it has been accepted by the Product Owner during the Sprint Review meeting.

Note: For some Product Development focused organizations, their Product Backlog may never be completed. This renders the effectiveness of the Burn-Up Chart useless. In this case, the Product Owner may decide to shift the context of the Burn-Up Chart to the next Release. As a Release Burn-Up Chart, the Product Owner can have an effective tool to keep the Team focused on delivering exactly what is needed to hit the targeted release.

Context

The entire Product Development effort

Setup

X Axis: The total number of Sprints

Y Axis: The Size of the Product Backlog (typically measured in Story Points, but you can simply count the Product Backlog Items as well)

What Is Plotted

The Blue Line: Shows the current size of the Product Backlog in Story Points (or count of the Product Backlog Items in the Product Backlog)

The Red Line: Shows the cumulative total of Story Points (or Product Backlog Items) earned (i.e. The Product Owner has accepted the Product Backlog Items during the Sprint Review Meeting)

The Green Line (Optional): Show the Team's Velocity, Sprint-over-Sprint

Responsible Party

The Product Owner: A fully committed Product Owner, who cares about the progress of the Team will typically take ownership for updating the Burn-Up Chart each Sprint.

The ScrumMaster: If the Product Owner is too busy or delegates the responsibility, it may fall on the ScrumMaster to update the Burn-Up Chart each Sprint.

Smells (Problems For The Burn-Up Chart)

Smell 1: One of the major issues that may limit the effectiveness of the Burn-Up Chart is a Team that doesn't size the entire Product Backlog. Many Teams end up only sizing the work to be completed during the Sprint in the Sprint Planning meeting. This is too late and limits the Product Owners effectiveness. It's well worth it to spend the time up-front to Size the entire Product Backlog as it is being seeded. This practice makes a tool like the Burn-Up Chart possible.

Smell 2: Everyone likes to look for patterns and try to be predictive. However, trying to predict the growth of the Product Backlog is not possible, because it's random. The best that we can do is look at the data we have at any given moment and make the best possible decisions. Any growth in the Product Backlog can be analyzed and the impact can be addressed with the Stakeholders. Avoid the trap of trying to be a fortune teller.

Smell 3: With any chart in Agile, it is critical to include an appropriate xplanation of what it means. An uninformed Stakeholder, who isn't prepared for 1e Product Backlog to grow over time, may be in for a shock when they find out 1at has occurred in the very next Sprint. Be sure to explain the Empirical nature of crum and how growth of the Product Backlog is not only expected, but also elcomed over time. Armed with this information, Stakeholders can then make 1ore informed decisions about how to use the information being presented by the roduct Owner with the Burn-Up Chart.

Burn-Down Chart

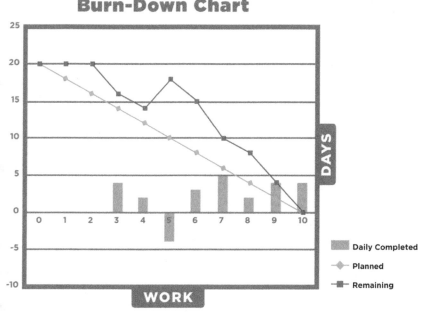

Definition and Usage

1e **Burn-Down Chart** is a graphical depiction of the planned work versus the ork remaining on a daily basis in a Sprint. It is a tactical tool, utilized by the Team, see if they are on-track to reach their Sprint Goal on a daily basis. Typically viewed at each Daily Scrum, the Team gets a real-time view of their progress. It a very useful tool, utilized by most Scrum Teams. Almost all tools built for Agile velopment include some type of Burn-Down Chart functionality.

Context

1e Sprint

X Axis: The number of days in the Sprint

Y Axis: Work; either measured as the summation of all the hours associated with every Task in the Sprint Backlog (preferred) or a count of the number of Tasks

The Blue Line: Shows the planned progress; every day we should Burn-Down a consistent number of hours/tasks, to reach zero by the end of the Sprint

The Red Line: Shows the work remaining, day-by-day

Responsible Party

The Team: It is our preference to see the Team taking ownership of creating and maintaining the Burn-Down chart. When the Team takes responsibility, they are truly seeing the value of the tool and are fully committed to knowing their progress on a daily basis.

The ScrumMaster: It is not uncommon to see the ScrumMaster assume the responsibility for creating and maintaining the Burn-Down chart. If this is your reality, the ScrumMaster should be careful not to hound the Team for data, because it can easily be perceived as micro-managing the Team.

Smells (Problems For The Burn-Down Chart)

Smell 1: Mentioned above, if the ScrumMaster is responsible for compiling the Burn-Down Chart for the Team, be careful when setting up the process for collecting data. You want a push system, rather than a pull system, that way the Team doesn't start feeling micro-managed.

Smell 2: The Burn-Down Chart is a tactical tool primarily utilized by the Team. When sharing it with others, it is important to set proper context. If management views the chart, and the progress of the Team is less than ideal, they may be inclined to swoop in and rescue the Team from themselves, which should be avoided at all costs.

Smell 3: Sometimes Teams will plot the summation of the *Story Points* (or count of User Stories) instead of the summation of the Task hours (or count of Tasks). While this view can be a useful addition, by itself it may not be very useful to the Team. The reason being is that a Team's typical pattern is to finish all the User Stories toward the end of the Sprint, leading to the Burn-Down chart displaying the infamous hockey stick pattern.

Scrum Board

To Do	In Progress	Ready For Review	Done
B			T T
B	T T	T T	
B	T T		
B T			

B =Backlog Item   **T** =Backlog Item

Definition and Usage

Kanban (pronounced kahn-bahn) is a word of Japanese origin that literally means "signboard." Its application in Agile/Scrum is as an **Information Radiator** and way of highlighting Task status within a Sprint. Kanban boards, also called **Scrum Boards** or Task Boards, are roughly designed into simple columns depicting the current state of any particular Product Backlog Item/Task. As a Task passes from one state to another, it moves horizontally from left to right along the Scrum Board. By graphically representing the state of each Task in the Sprint, everyone (Scrum Team and Stakeholders) can get an instant view of the progress (or lack of progress) being made in the Sprint.

Context

The Sprint

Setup

Every Scrum Board is unique, like snowflakes. What to show on the Scrum Board should be a Team-based decision.

Scrum Boards can be as basic as "To Do, Doing, & Done" or more complicated based on what the Team needs in order to be successful

The correct placement of the physical Scrum Board is key. Scrum Boards should be located near the Team's working area, but also in plain view and easy access of the Product Owner, ScrumMaster, and Stakeholders. Note: If your Team is distributed, there are electronic versions of Scrum Boards available as well.

Responsible Party

The Team

Smells (Problems For The Scrum Board)

Smell 1: The intent of Scrum is not to perform mini-waterfalls (requirement design, develop, and test) inside of Sprints, but rather to have the entire Team swarm (find ways to work together and do steps of the development process concurrently). Teams sometimes have tendencies to get too detailed by creating to many states on their Scrum Board. Try to coach the Team with the mantra "less is more" and see how few columns are really needed.

Smell 2: Teams lacking ownership of their Scrum Board may fight the need to update it. The ScrumMaster may find themself nagging the Team to complete their updates. The ScrumMaster doesn't like nagging and the Team starts to feel micro-managed. In order to resolve this issue, first identify if the Team had a say in the creation of their Scrum Board. If the design of the board was done by someone else, such as the ScrumMaster, then they may have less buy-in. If this is the case, the ScrumMaster should hold a Retrospective on the Scrum Board and let the Team re-design it. Another suggestion, if that doesn't work, is to have the Team complete their updates to the Scrum Board during the Daily Scrum meeting. The Team can move their tasks as they are answering the three questions. Updating the Scrum Board during the meeting forms a new habit and creates muscle memory. In time, the ScrumMaster should no longer need to remind the Team to update the Scrum Board

Smell 3: There isn't anything wrong with tools per say, (this book was written in Microsoft Word because it was more efficient than writing it by hand), but we must be careful when using them. Granting your Stakeholders access to your Scrum Board via your tool is a good idea, but expecting them to login and use it frequently isn't. A best practice is to mount one or more large video monitors around your office and project the Team's Scrum Board 24x7. Find ways to push out the information contained on the Scrum Board, rather than requiring people to pull it or risk the tool becoming an information refrigerator.

ARTIFACTS IN SCRUM SUMMARY—WHERE WE HAVE BEEN

This section explained the following primary and additional artifacts in Scrum:

Core Scrum Artifacts

Product Backlog, the overall list of everything we would like to accomplish

Sprint Backlog, the subset of the Product Backlog the Team feels comfortable committing to completing in the current Sprint

Product Increment, the accumulation of completed Product Backlog Items completed in one or more Sprints

Additional Scrum Artifacts

Velocity, a measure of how much work the Team is completing in a given Sprint. It is a great predictor of how much work the Team can accomplish in future Sprints

Burn-Up Charts, a favorite tool of the Product Owner to get a top-down view of how much remains in their Product (Or Release) Backlog and how much longer it will take to complete the Product.

Burn-Down Charts, a tactical tool used by Teams daily to know whether they are on track to meet their Spring Goal.

Scrum Boards, a great way to visually depict the work to be completed in the Sprint and serve as a real-time reminder of progress.

SUMMARY

Wow, you're still reading? Just kidding! Congratulations are in order for making it to the end of the book. We have covered a lot of ground in a short amount of time. Here is a brief re-cap of where we have been.

We started our journey together by taking a look at Scrum's roots in Agile. I gave you some ammo in the features and benefits section to use when trying to convince others to try Scrum. We even looked at an overview of Scrum and when it should be applied.

Next we turned our attention to the roles within Scrum. We saw how small, cross-functional Teams are able to self-organize and self-manage to get their work done. We learned of how the business gets engaged with the Product Development effort by appointing a Product Owner. Last, but not least, we saw how the Scrum Team is rounded out by the inclusion of our process mentor, the ScrumMaster. Also, we learned about the Chickens (Stakeholders) and how to best meet their needs.

Our journey continued with an in-depth look at the key meetings in the Scrum process. Each Sprint starts with a Sprint Planning meeting, where the Scrum Team focuses on the "What" and "How" conversations to scope their work for the next two to four weeks. We learned about the heartbeat of the Sprint, through the Daily Scrum (Daily Standup). How, along the way, we need to take time out of our current Sprint to refine our Product Backlog, breaking down Product Backlog Items into manageable chunks of work. Best of all, we learned about the need to inspect and adapt the Product in the Sprint Review and the process in the Sprint Retrospective.

Our last major content area was the primary and secondary artifacts in Scrum. "We don't need no stinking documentation", you say? Not true, we definitely need a Product Backlog, multiple Product Backlogs, and our Stakeholders sure want that Product Increment. We also learned how to increase the transparency of our efforts by tracking our Velocity, measure our progress using Burn-Up and Burn-Down charts, and always know where we stand by looking at our Scrum Board.

Whew, that was a lot of ground and I am now very tired of typing. I am sure that you are tired of reading too. Go grab a cup of coffee, you have earned it!

WHERE DO YOU GO FROM HERE?

They say that knowledge is the great equalizer. That's true, but having a base level understanding of Scrum is just the start. There is so much more to learn along your journey. Some things you can pick up from reading, others will need to be learned from experience. I highly encourage you to go out there and practice Scrum. Don't be afraid to mess it up - experiment, play, and, most importantly, have fun!

FINAL, FINAL THOUGHT

I truly hope this book helps you in your noble quest to improve your life and those around you. My personal slogan is, "Passionately helping others grow". I hope you felt my passion come through in these pages and hope my passion is contagious. Go out there and make something happen, fight the good fight, and never give up hope for a better tomorrow!

Sincerely,

Brian Rabon

Brian M. Rabon, CST, PMP

P.S. There is a very useful glossary coming up next. It's full of every Agile/Scrum term in this book.

P.P.S. Did you like this book? If so, buy another copy and give it to a friend or co-worker. When everyone is on the same level playing field of understanding, we all win!

GLOSSARY

Look here to find definitions for all of the Bolded and Italicized terms in this guide.

Acceptance Criteria—Prior to implementing a Product Backlog Item, the Team and Product Owner mutually agree upon what it means to be Done.

Adapt—Being willing to change direction (deviate from plan), when new and better information surfaces (being Agile)

Agile—A mindset or a philosophy for working, characterized by the 4 values and 12 principles in the Agile Manifesto

Agile Manifesto—A unifying statement of "why" the founding fathers of Agile created their methods. Checkout http://www.agilemanifesto.org for more information.

Backlog Item—See Product Backlog Item

Burn-Down Chart—A graphical depiction of the planned work vs work remaining in the context of a Sprint. It helps the Scrum Team understand, on a daily basis, if they are on-track to meet their Sprint Goal.

Burn-Up Chart—A graphical depiction of the Size of the Product Backlog Items in the Product backlog vs how many Product Backlog Items the Team has completed. Often used by the Product Owner to forecast possible completion dates for the Stakeholders

Business Value—A fundamental Agile measure. Does the item in question have a value to the business (I.e. is it worth implementing from a hard or soft benefit perspective)?

Capacity—See Velocity

Chickens—In Scrum, the Stakeholders and Stakeholders alone are considered Chickens because of what they bring to the table. Stakeholders bring their ideas, suggestions, and criticisms making them involved, but not committed to the Product development effort.

Cross-Functional—All the skill sets necessary to build the Product, located within one Team.

Defined—The belief that all variables can be known up-front (known inputs, peatable process, and expected outputs) as opposed to Emperically.

emo—A brief "show and tell" of a Potentially Shippable Product Increment

one (Definition of)—When a Product Backlog Item has reached a "production" eady state (able to be used by the Stakeholders)

mpirical—Create Transparency then Inspect and Adapt along the way

pic—Any Product Backlog Item too big to be completed in a single Sprint

igh-Bandwidth Communication—Meeting face-to-face allows us to communicate ore information; not only do we have our words, but also the pitch and tone of our ice in addition to our body language.

leal Hours—A unit of measure representing the amount of time (in hours) it ould take to complete a Task.

formation Radiator—A term coined by Alistair Cockburn to describe "big-visible arts"

spect—Evaluate what is going on and decide if it is good or bad

tegration—Making sure the newly produced Product Backlog Items fit together d play nicely with the existing features in the Product Increment

eration—A brief Timebox, typically two weeks, when a team of individuals work produce a Potentially Shippable Product Increment. It's a generic Agile term.

rdered—There is debate in the Scrum community about whether the Product cklog is Prioritized or Ordered (Ordered being more all inclusive of other ctors). Perhaps we are just a little traditional, but we like Prioritized better.

gs—The Scrum Team because they are fully ommitted" to the Product development effort

tentially Shippable—The Product Increment Done and is now a business decision for the oduct Owner to make as to whether it should to Production.

iority—A complex set of criteria determining e order in which the Team implements oduct Backlog Items.

Product—What the Stakeholders are paying for and the Team is building

Product Backlog Item—A single feature, change request, or bug/defect for the Product

Product Backlog Refinement—Working one or two Sprints ahead on refining Product Backlog Items and the top of the Product Backlog

Product Backlog Seeding—A process by which the Product Owner holds sessions with various groups of Stakeholders and Scrum Team Members to author Product Backlog Items for the Product Backlog

Product Increment—A fully functional piece of the Product, composed of one or more Product Backlog Items

Product Owner—A single business representative who builds consensus and represents the needs, wants, and desires of the Stakeholders to the Team

Product Roadmap—Often created by the Product Owner with the help of key Stakeholders, a Product Roadmap prioritizes business goals and priorities

Production—A state where the Product is being actively used by the Stakeholders

Production Ready—When the Product has reached a state of Done, the goal of every Sprint is to produce a Product Increment that is Production Ready

Ready (Definition of)—A Product Backlog Item is deemed Ready by the Team when it has been refined sufficiently to fit within the context of a single Sprint

Relative Estimate—An estimate not based upon time, but rather the complexity of implementing one Product Backlog Item as compared to implementing another one

Release Plan—Sprints conclude with a Potentially Shippable Product Increment then become a business decision as to when to ship the Product to the Stakeholder Therefore, a Release Plan is a best guess as to when and what functionality will be put into Production.

Return On Investment (ROI)—The expected benefit to be received when a Produ Backlog Item is put into Production, often equated in monetary figures

Roadblock—Any risk or issue impeding the Team's forward progress

Scrum—A "way to get work done" that is Agile and follows the Empirical type to working

Scrum Board—A form of an Information Radiator, a Scrum Board is a graphical depiction of the work state for each Task in the current Sprint

Scrum Board

To Do	In Progress	Ready For Review	Done
B			T T
B	T T	T T	
B	T T		
B T			

B =Backlog Item   T =Backlog Item

Self-Managing—We consider the Team to be Self-Managing when they learn to take ownership of their work and issues and can function without the need for outside direction telling them what to do and how to do it.

Self-Organizing—We consider the Team to be Self-Organizing when the individual Team Members chose the work they would like to do, rather than having it chosen for them. This allows individuals to work outside of the subject matter domain and cross-train in other areas.

Servant Leadership—The recommended leadership style to be practiced in an Agile environment. Servant Leadership is based upon the premise that in order to lead we must first be willing to serve.

Sizing—See Relative Estimate

Specializing Generalist—Someone who is highly skilled in one or two areas, but also comfortable working in several areas where they are not an expert

Sprint—A 2 to 4 week period of time, during which the Team produces a Potentially Shippable Product Increment

Sprint Backlog—The subset of the Product Backlog (Product Backlog Items) selected by the Product Owner and Team and the Tasks created by the Team for accomplishing those items to be developed in the current Sprint

Sprint Goal—The unifying "theme" of the Sprint (e.g. We are focused on reporting this Sprint). Sprint Goals are important because they tie the work of the Sprint back to the Product Roadmap and help us communicate what we are working on to our Stakeholders.

Sprint Planning—The meeting at the beginning of every Sprint where the "What" and the "How" (Sprint Backlog) are defined for the Sprint

Stakeholders—Anyone impacted by the Product the Scrum Team is producing. This includes management, subject matter experts, and customers

Story Points—An abstract measure used for Relative Estimation/Sizing, typically represented as a sequence of numbers such as the Binary (1, 2, 4, 8, 16, 32,...) or Fibonacci Sequence (0, 1, 2 , 3, 5, 8,...)

Task—A discrete piece of work that can be completed in 2 to 4 hours

Team—A group of 5 to 9 (7 +/-2) Team Members

Team Member—An individual contributor on a Team; Team Members check their title at the door and are willing to do whatever it takes to help the Team succeed, even if that means doing something outside of their skill set or comfort zone.

Technical Debt—Taking shortcuts when developing a Product Backlog Item that cause underlying issues. These issues re-surface in Production and can cause the Product to not function properly. Technical Debt is typically cheaper to pay down early in the Sprint, where issues found in Production can be very costly to resolve.

Technobabble—Using technical language and jargon in an effort to create confusion and make others who do not know the terms feel inferior or stupid

Timebox—A set period of time

The Scrum Team—The Team Members, Product Owner, and ScrumMaster, collectively

Transparency—Making things visible for all to see, not hiding anything

User Story—Not a "Scrum" term, more of an Agile best practice; User Stories are short, three sentence placeholders for requirements. As a..., I want..., so that... is the format of a User Story (e.g., As a swimmer, I want a salt water filtration system, so that my hair doesn't turn green.). It's common to refer to the three C's of a User tory: the card, conformation, and the conversation. The card is the "As a, I want, to that"; the conformation is the Acceptance Criteria; and the conversation is a reminder to have a chat before implementing it.

Value Stream—The steps of your development process directly contributing to delivering value to your Stakeholders.

Velocity—A historical measure of how much work was accomplished within the Sprint, typically measured in Story Points. Knowing a Team's Velocity helps in a number of ways; Product Owners can be more predictive with Burn-Up Charts and Release Planning and Teams can be more predictive of how much work can be accomplished in a given Sprint.

Vision—The Product's Elevator Pitch, a 30 second commercial for what we are doing and why we are doing it

Waterfall—A traditional, plan-driven development method. In Waterfall, work is done in phases and typically handed off to separate groups for completion. A typical Waterfall cycle is; requirements, design, develop, test, and deploy.

Yesterday's Weather—A planning technique used by Scrum Teams to estimate their Velocity for the current Sprint. To apply Yesterday's Weather, simply use the Velocity from the last Sprint to plan for the current one.

ABOUT THE AUTHOR

Brian M. Rabon, CST, PMP is an IT professional with over 16 years of industry experience. Brian holds a Bachelor's Degree in Computer Science from Auburn University and a Master's Degree in Electrical Engineering from the University of Alabama at Birmingham's Information Engineering and Management program.

Brian is President of The Braintrust Consulting Group, a worldwide leader in Agile transformations. Through practical, hands-on training and enterprise and Team coaching, Brian helps his clients learn, plan, and implement Agile processes, such as Scrum and Kanban. His goal is to teach his clients how to increase predictability of delivery, decrease time-to-market, and improve overall client satisfaction.

When not in the classroom, Brian can be found around the globe evangelizing the benefits of Agile to the likes of conferences such as Agile 20XX, the Project Management Institute's (PMI) many Chapter symposiums and professional development days, and the Scrum Alliance's Scrum Gatherings. Brian is a founding member of Agile Birmingham, a current member of PMI Northern Utah Chapter, and a professional member of the National Speakers Association (NSA).

Brian does laundry in Salt Lake City, UT where he ocassional sees his beautiful wif Elizabeth, and their miniature schnauzer, Madison. Brian occasionally finds time to enjoy his summer passion of relaxing at the beach and his winter passion of snow skiing.

Brian's Contact Information

brian.rabon@braintrustgroup.com

LinkedIn: http://www.linkedin.com/in/bmrabon

205.329.3794

ABOUT THE BRAINTRUST CONSULTING GROUP

The Braintrust Consulting Group is a worldwide leader in Agile transformations. Through practical, hands-on training and enterprise and Team coaching, we help our clients learn, plan, and implement Agile processes, such as Scrum and Kanban.

We would love to have you join the conversation and stay in touch with us. We aren't hard to find on the interweb.

Blog: http://www.braintrustgroup.com/blog

Facebook: http://www.facebook.com/braintrustgroup

Google+: http://gplus.to/braintrustgroup

LinkedIn: http://www.linkedin.com/company/the-braintrust-consulting-group

Slideshare: http://www.slideshare.net/yourpmpartner

Twitter: https://twitter.com/braintrustgroup

Vimeo: http://vimeo.com/braintrustgroup

Website: http://www.braintrustgroup.com

YouTube: http://www.youtube.com/user/yourpmpartner

Contact Information

1978 Montgomery Highway South
Suite 104 #237
Dover, AL 35216

5.757.6017

info@braintrustgroup.com

TRAINING

If you are looking for a boring, classroom lecture where you can take a nap and earn PDUs, then you are in the wrong place. If you think that manufacturing the world's best paper airplanes by following the latest in proven Scrum techniques sounds like fun, then you are in the right place.

Our approach to training at The Braintrust Consulting Group can be summed up in two words...

ENERGETIC AND ENGAGING

At The Braintrust Consulting Group, we are passionate about Agile and it shows in every class we teach. We not only teach Agile, we live and breathe it. Our unique approach to training focuses on hands-on-exercises and utilizes the latest brain science techniques from the field of Accelerated Learning. No matter which one of our classes you attend, you will be entertained, challenged, and engaged. We guarantee you will leave with a new set of skills, ready to be applied immediately and have fun doing so!

We offer the following training options:

Certified Scrum Training

Certified Scrum Developer (CSD)

Agile Engineering

Test Driven Development

Certified ScrumMaster (CSM)

Certified Scrum Product Owner (CSPO)

Non-Certified Agile/Scrum Training

Kanban Essentials

Scrum Essentials

User Story Writing Workshop

Public Class Schedule: http://www.braintrustgroup.com/classes/upcoming

Testimonials: http://braintrustgroup.com/case-studies/testimonials

COACHING

When adopting Agile methods, a trusted advisor can save your Team time and frustration. At The Braintrust Consulting Group, we know that the best way to support clients during a Scrum implementation is with coaching. Our experienced coaches will work with you to assess your specific needs and create a customized implementation plan. With a plan in place, we can then tailor our services to your Team's unique challenges. We offer the following coaching options:

Level 1—Agile/Scrum Evaluation

Agile/Scrum Evaluation is ideal for companies who are already following an Agile or Scrum process, but are looking for an external coach to audit their process and identify ways to improve efficiency and effectiveness. Within this coaching program, our expert coaches will perform a 360-degree retrospective with your Team, your business partners, and your Stakeholders. The goal of Agile/Scrum Evaluation Coaching is to evaluate and document the current usage of Agile, identify knowledge gaps, and recommend areas for improvement.

Level 2—Agile/Scrum Kickstart

Agile/Scrum Kickstart is ideal for companies who have invested in Agile/Scrum training, and are planning to implement an Agile process, but have limited time or budget. Our Agile/Scrum Kickstart program is designed to help your Team implement Agile/Scrum in the real world. Our expert coaches provide guidance through the implementation process and get your Team up to speed faster and with less miss-starts.

Level 3—Custom Agile/Scrum Coaching

Custom coaching is our most comprehensive level of coaching. It is ideal for companies who want to maximize their success with Agile on a larger, organization-wide scale. Under our Custom Agile/Scrum Coaching, we will create an individualized plan for your organization based on your structure, goals, and challenges. Through a combination of in-person and over-the-phone sessions, our expert coaches will guide your Team, your Stakeholders, and your business leaders through every step of the Agile/Scrum adoption process with a focus on knowledge transfer. We believe in teaching your Team to fish, not constantly handing you one. Our goal is to lead your Team through a transformation resulting in a culture and environment capable of self-replication and organic growth.

More information on our coaching services : http://braintrustgroup.com/coaching-approach

Video Case Studies: http://braintrustgroup.com/case-studies/agile-case-study

Testimonials: http://braintrustgroup.com/case-studies/testimonials

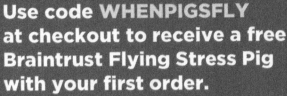

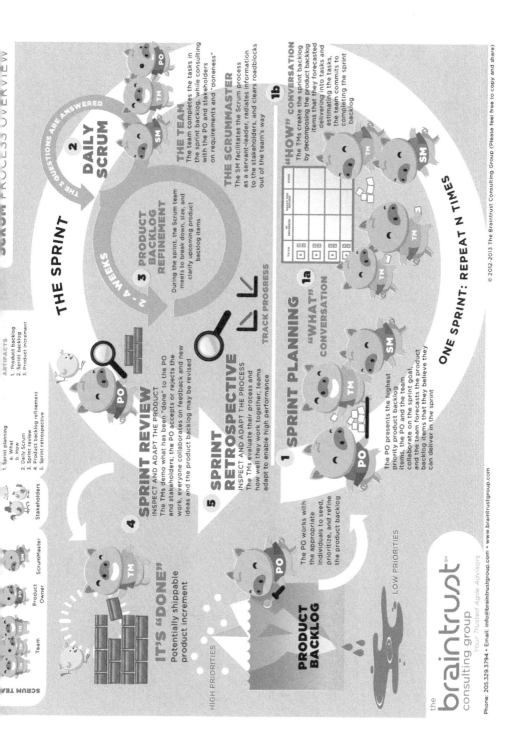

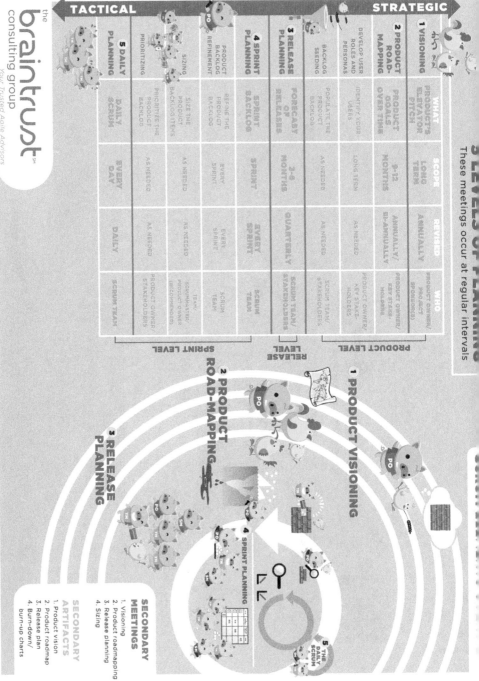

TACTICAL ← → **STRATEGIC**

3 LEVELS OF PLANNING
These meetings occur at regular intervals

	WHAT	SCOPE	REVISED	WHO
PRODUCT LEVEL				
1 VISIONING	PRODUCT'S ELEVATOR PITCH	LONG TERM	ANNUALLY	PRODUCT OWNER/ PROJECT (SPONSORS)
2 PRODUCT ROAD-MAPPING	PRODUCT GOALS OVER TIME	9-12 MONTHS	ANNUALLY/ BI-ANNUALLY	PRODUCT OWNER/ KEY STAKE-HOLDERS
DEVELOP USER ROLES AND PERSONAS	IDENTIFY YOUR USERS	LONG TERM	AS NEEDED	PRODUCT OWNER/ KEY STAKE-HOLDERS
BACKLOG SEEDING	POPULATE THE PRODUCT BACKLOG	AS NEEDED	AS NEEDED	SCRUM TEAM/ STAKEHOLDERS
RELEASE LEVEL				
3 RELEASE PLANNING	FORECAST OF RELEASES	3-6 MONTHS	QUARTERLY	SCRUM TEAM/ STAKEHOLDERS
SPRINT LEVEL				
4 SPRINT PLANNING	SPRINT BACKLOG	SPRINT	EVERY SPRINT	SCRUM TEAM
PRODUCT BACKLOG REFINEMENT	REFINE THE PRODUCT BACKLOG	EVERY SPRINT	EVERY SPRINT	SCRUM TEAM
SIZING	SIZE THE PRODUCT BACKLOG	AS NEEDED	AS NEEDED	TEAM/ SCRUMMASTER/ PRODUCT OWNER (RECOMMENDED)
PRIORITIZING	PRIORITIZE THE PRODUCT BACKLOG	AS NEEDED	AS NEEDED	PRODUCT OWNER/ STAKEHOLDERS
5 DAILY PLANNING	DAILY SCRUM	EVERY DAY	DAILY	SCRUM TEAM

1 PRODUCT VISIONING

2 PRODUCT ROAD-MAPPING

3 RELEASE PLANNING

4 SPRINT PLANNING

5 THE DAILY SCRUM

SECONDARY MEETINGS
1. Visioning
2. Product roadmapping
3. Release planning
4. Sizing

SECONDARY ARTIFACTS
1. Product vision
2. Product roadmap
3. Release plan
4. Burn-down/ burn-up charts

NOTES

CPSIA information can be obtained at www.ICGtesting.com
Printed in the USA
BVOW10s0526280115

385250BV00003B/3/P